CHURCHES OF LINCOLNSHIRE

JOHN E. VIGAR

AMBERLEY

Front cover: Haltham-on-Bain. *Rear cover*: Waithe.

This edition first published 2026

Amberley Publishing
The Hill, Stroud
Gloucestershire GL5 4EP

www.amberley-books.com

British Library Cataloguing in Publication Data.
A catalogue record for this book is available from the British Library.

ISBN 978 1 3981 2728 9 (print)
ISBN 978 1 3981 2729 6 (ebook)

Typesetting by SJmagic DESIGN SERVICES, India.
Printed in Great Britain.

Appointed GPSR EU Representative: Easy Access System Europe Oü, 16879218
Address: Mustamäe tee 50, 10621, Tallinn, Estonia
Contact Details: gpsr.requests@easproject.com, +358 40 500 3575

Contents

Map 4

Key 5

Introduction 6

1. Ancaster, St Martin 6
2. Bigby, All Saints 7
3. Bloxholm, St Mary 9
4. Boston, St Botolph 11
5. Brant Broughton, St Helen 13
6. Bratoft, St Peter and St Paul 15
7. Brocklesby, All Saints 18
8. Burgh le Marsh, St Peter and St Paul 19
9. Burton upon Stather, St Andrew 21
10. Burwell, St Michael 22
11. Burton Coggles, St Thomas Becket 24
12. Caythorpe, St Vincent 26
13. Claypole, St Peter 28
14. Coates, St Edith 31
15. Crowle, St Oswald 33
16. Deeping St James, Priory Church of St James 35
17. Denton, St Andrew 37
18. Donington, St Mary and the Holy Rood 39
19. Edenham, St Michael 41
20. Gautby, All Saints 43
21. Gedney, St Mary Magdalene 45
22. Grantham, St Wulfram 48
23. Hainton, St Mary 50
24. Haltham-on-Bain, St Benedict 52
25. Halton Holegate, St Andrew 54
26. Hannah cum Hagnaby, St Andrew 56
27. Ingoldmells, St Peter and St Paul 58
28. Ingoldsby, St Bartholomew 60
29. Kingerby, St Peter 61
30. Kirmington, St Helen 63
31. Langton by Spilsby, St Peter and St Paul 65
32. Louth, St James 67
33. Navenby, St Peter 69
34. Normanby le Wold, St Peter 71
35. Oxcombe, All Saints 72
36. Pickworth, St Andrew 74
37. Quadring, St Margaret 76
38. Redbourne, St Andrew 78
39. Saltfleetby, All Saints 80
40. Scotton, St Genewys 82
41. Sleaford, St Denys 84
42. Snarford, St Lawrence 86
43. Snitterby, St Nicholas 88
44. Spilsby, St James 89
45. Stamford, St Martin 90
46. Stoke Rochford, St Mary and St Andrew 91
47. Tattershall, Holy Trinity 92
48. Waithe, St Martin 94
49. West Keal, St Helen 95

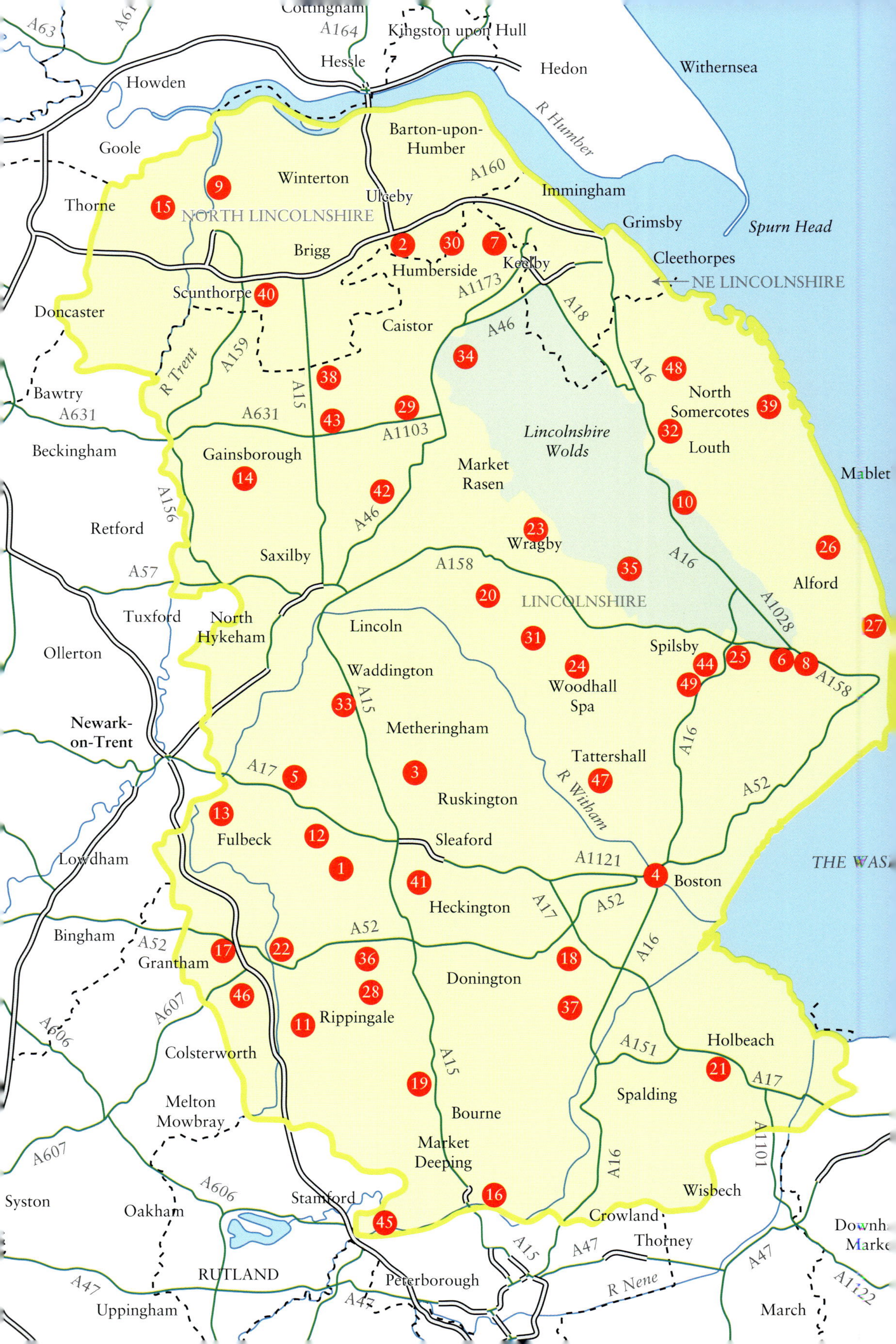

A63
A164
Kingston upon Hull
Hessle
Hedon
Withernsea
Howden
R Humber
Goole
Barton-upon-Humber
Winterton
A160
Immingham
Thorne
Ulceby
NORTH LINCOLNSHIRE
Grimsby
Spurn Head
Brigg
Humberside
Keelby
Cleethorpes
Scunthorpe
A1173
NE LINCOLNSHIRE
Doncaster
A18
A46
Caistor
R Trent
A159
A16
Bawtry
A15
North Somercotes
A631
A631
A1103
Beckingham
Lincolnshire Wolds
Louth
Gainsborough
Market Rasen
Mablet
A156
A46
Retford
Wragby
Saxilby
A16
A57
A158
Alford
LINCOLNSHIRE
A1028
Tuxford
North Hykeham
Lincoln
Ollerton
Spilsby
Waddington
A15
A158
Woodhall Spa
Newark-on-Trent
Metheringham
A16
Tattershall
A17
R Witham
Ruskington
A52
Fulbeck
Sleaford
Lowdham
A1121
Boston
Heckington
A17
A52
Bingham
A52
A52
Grantham
A16
Donington
A607
A606
Rippingale
A151
Holbeach
Colsterworth
A15
A17
Melton Mowbray
Spalding
Bourne
A1101
A607
Market Deeping
A16
A606
Syston
Stamford
Wisbech
Oakham
Crowland
A15
A47
Thorney
RUTLAND
A47
A47
R Nene
Peterborough
A1122
Uppingham
A47
March
1
2
3
4
5
6
7
8
9
10
11
12
13
14
15
16
17
18
19
20
21
22
23
24
25
26
27
28
29
30
31
32
33
34
35
36
37
38
39
40
41
42
43
44
45
46
47
48
49

Key

1. Ancaster, St Martin
2. Bigby, All Saints
3. Bloxholm, St Mary
4. Boston, St Botolph
5. Brant Broughton, St Helen
6. Bratoft, St Peter and St Paul
7. Brocklesby, All Saints
8. Burgh le Marsh, St Peter and St Paul
9. Burton upon Stather, St Andrew
10. Burwell, St Michael
11. Burton Coggles, St Thomas Becket
12. Caythorpe, St Vincent
13. Claypole, St Peter
14. Coates, St Edith
15. Crowle, St Oswald
16. Deeping St James, Priory Church of St James
17. Denton, St Andrew
18. Donington, St Mary and the Holy Rood
19. Edenham, St Michael
20. Gautby, All Saints
21. Gedney, St Mary Magdalene
22. Grantham, St Wulfram
23. Hainton, St Mary
24. Haltham-on-Bain, St Benedict
25. Halton Holegate, St Andrew
26. Hannah cum Hagnaby, St Andrew
27. Ingoldmells, St Peter and St Paul
28. Ingoldsby, St Bartholomew
29. Kingerby, St Peter
30. Kirmington, St Helen
31. Langton by Spilsby, St Peter and St Paul
32. Louth, St James
33. Navenby, St Peter
34. Normanby le Wold, St Peter
35. Oxcombe, All Saints
36. Pickworth, St Andrew
37. Quadring, St Margaret
38. Redbourne, St Andrew
39. Saltfleetby, All Saints
40. Scotton, St Genewys
41. Sleaford, St Denys
42. Snarford, St Lawrence
43. Snitterby, St Nicholas
44. Spilsby, St James
45. Stamford, St Martin
46. Stoke Rochford, St Mary and St Andrew
47. Tattershall, Holy Trinity
48. Waithe, St Martin
49. West Keal, St Helen

Introduction

Lincolnshire is a large county and few visit unless they have business there. Until the opening of the Humber Bridge there were no through roads, so historically it has been little explored. Yet its legacy of historic churches is probably only matched by Norfolk, with churches that owe their very existence to maritime trade and wool production. Architecturally, it has benefitted from the influence of a myriad of monasteries and, of course, from its stunning cathedral. However, the wealth that created such a collection of large buildings also led to depopulation elsewhere, and tiny Norman churches remind us of those communities that didn't survive. The cyclical nature of history saw a repeat of this pattern in two later periods. First, when communities which had been supported by monastic landlords dispersed and migrated to towns and, more recently, when small-scale industrialisation reinvigorated some struggling rural villages. All these changes are represented in the parish churches of the county, which range from large Saxon structures at Barton-upon-Humber, tiny Norman churches like Coates by Stow, through grand wool churches at Swineshead and Gedney to the Georgian gem at Oxcombe. This book includes a selection of forty-nine characteristic buildings from across the county.

1. Ancaster, St Martin

The local limestone has been quarried for millennia and is found in buildings across England. Its earliest visible use here was by the Romans who built a town on Ermine Street and who constructed a shrine to the Mother Goddesses on the site of the present church. A reproduction of the shrine is displayed in the churchyard by the road. St Martin's has a Norman core. On the exterior of the north wall of the chancel is a corbel table, or course of decorative carvings common on twelfth-century buildings. It is not quite in its original position, but we are lucky that it was saved as successive generations altered the building. Inside, the north arcade is also Norman with round-headed arches of increasing complexity of decoration. They must have engaged different stonemasons, each trying to outdo his predecessor in building to 'the glory of God'. The font is of the same period – a circular drum with intersecting tracery. I love the east window of the north aisle which, despite its wonkiness, has amazing tracery of about 1300 with four mouchettes forming twin circles. The porch contains effigies of two fourteenth-century priests who must once have been in the chancel and who may have kept their books in the aumbry (cupboard), which is still there. There are few later monuments in the church, but one, a naïve trumpeting angel, is worthy of attention. It commemorates Elizabeth Long, who died in 1743. The inscription employs several different styles of lettering and the setting-out lines may be clearly seen. The designer must have been very proud of his work as he signed his name prominently at the bottom: Joshua Long – surely a relative of the deceased? Stained-glass windows have often been added to churches in an ad hoc way and in most instances notice was taken of subjects already used, so it is surprising that in such a small church the four evangelists appear twice. Their symbols appear in the chancel window, and they can be seen in portraits in the west window. Interestingly, they both commemorate members of the Allix family and date from almost the same year. If you have binoculars with you have a close look at the myriad of carvings on the tower. Not only is there a sexualised Sheela-na-gig, but a gentleman on the corner is relieving himself!

2. Bigby, All Saints

Here, the thirteenth-century church stands east end on to the road through the village, whilst the churchyard slopes prettily down to the west. We have come to see the interesting range of monuments inside. The sequence starts with a medieval lady, her hands in prayer. The rolls of fabric on her headdress tell us immediately that she was recut by the Victorians in an effort to make her more presentable. Then comes an incised slab to a lady of a couple of generations later, although being a flat floor slab means that she has been rather worn away; the inscription around the edge is barely readable. Elizabeth Skipwith has a brass effigy with inscription, although the latter is made up of two separate pieces of metal, possibly reusing brass from elsewhere. Sadly, it is being eaten into by bat urine. On the north side of the chancel are two important monuments. The earlier is to Robert Tyrwhit (d. 1581) and his wife Elizabeth Oxenbridge, together with their twenty-two children. Those who died as babies are depicted in swaddling clothes. Elizabeth's feet are guarded by a lion whilst her husband has a 'wodewose' (a wild man of the woods) at his feet happily playing with the rolled-up end of his palliass. Sadly, the top of his head has been sliced off, and the monument is in poor condition in part due to damp coming through the wall. Robert was a recusant Catholic and was imprisoned in the Fleet Prison in London in 1581 together with two of his sons. They were allowed out of prison to attend his funeral the following year. Nearby is the wall monument to another Robert Tyrwhit (d. 1617) and his wife Bridget Manners, daughter of the 4th Earl of Rutland. It shows them kneeling facing each other, and there would have been a prayer desk between them. Bridget was a favourite lady-in-waiting to Elizabeth I and when the time came for her to marry she couldn't bring herself to ask permission to leave court, so she made an excuse about her mother's ill health. Whilst away, she and Robert married, and when the queen found out she threw Robert in the Tower of London and demanded that half the dowry paid to his family should be given to her instead, after which Robert was released. The complicated heraldry above the tomb shows us Elizabeth's distinctive lineage. This sequence of monuments ends with a small rectangular brass plate to Edward Nayler (d. 1632), a rector here who is described

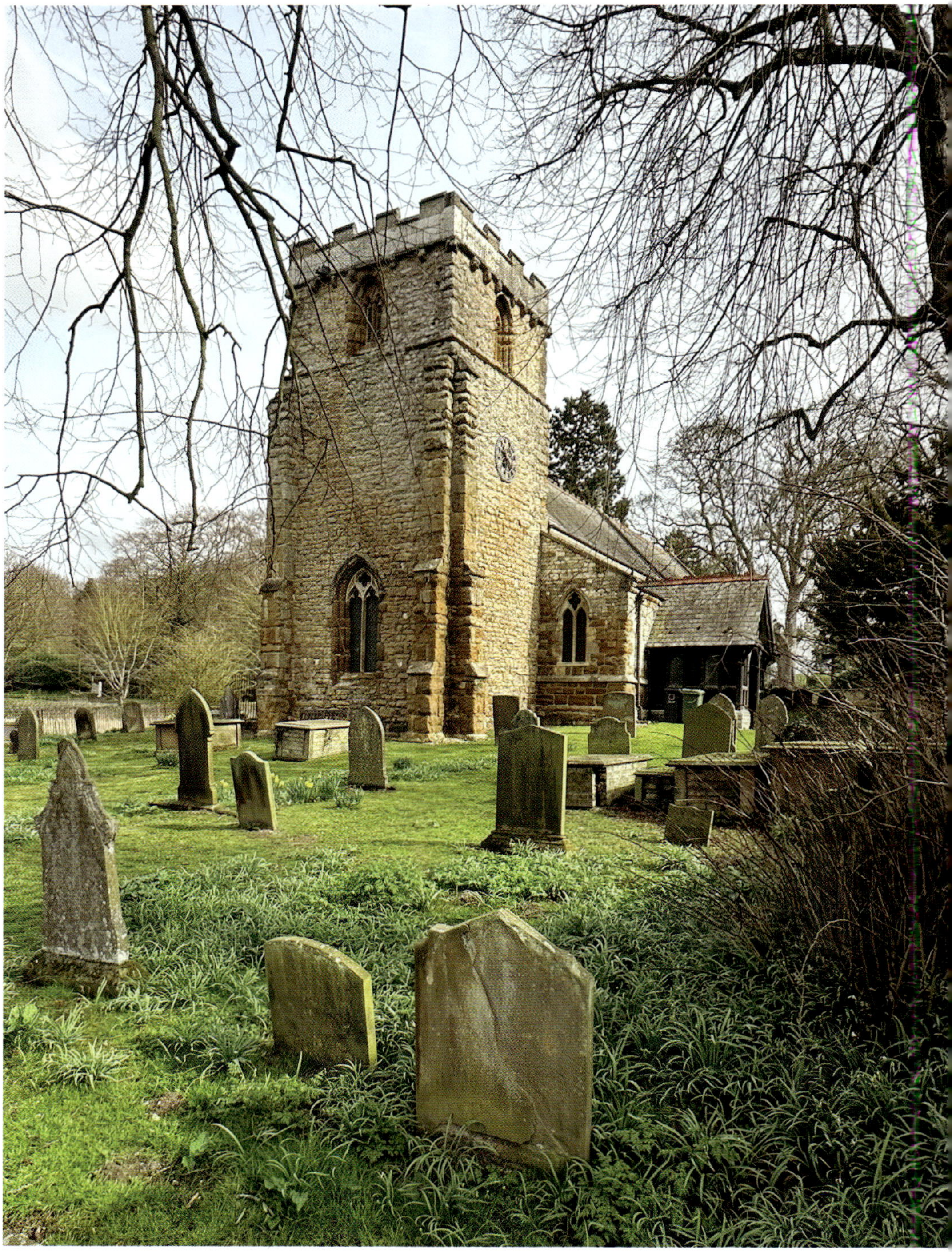

Bigby. The weather-worn sandstone walls of the west tower, with its clasping buttresses, dates from the thirteenth century. Below the battlements you can see a corbel table of carved heads.

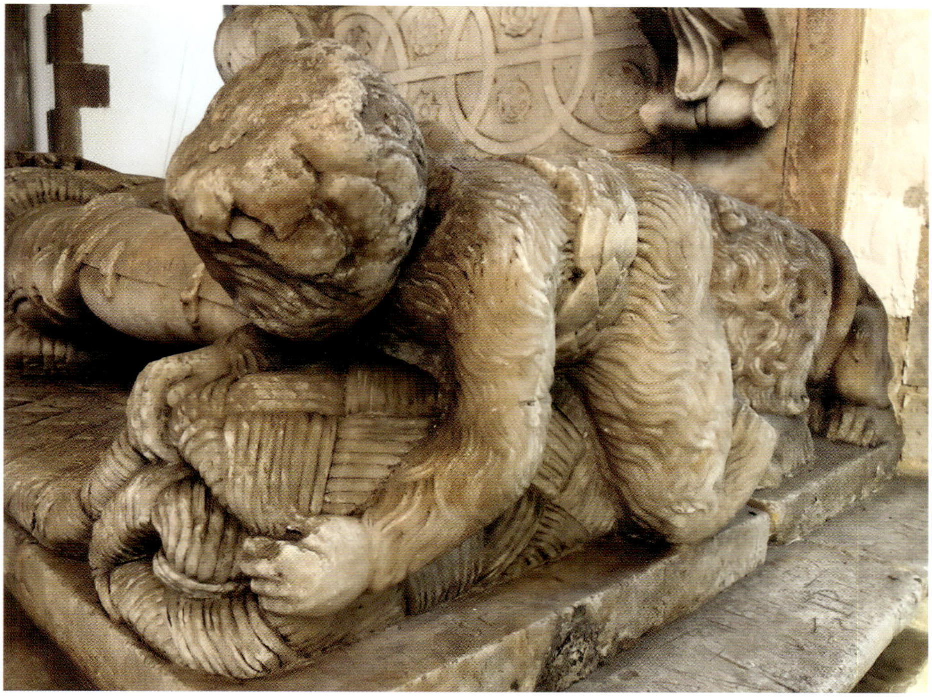

Bigby. A detail from the alabaster tomb of Sir Robert Tyrwhit, who died in 1581, shows a wodewose or wild man of the woods trying to unroll the mat at his feet.

as a 'painfulle minister of God's word'. His wife and seven children are depicted. It is thought that this brass may be by William Wright of Charing Cross, who was working at Brocklesby at the time (see entry 7). The inscription, especially the shapes of the numbers, is characteristically his and we know that he worked on brasses in other parts of the country, although this would be the earliest known.

3. Bloxholm, St Mary

A delightful small church in the meadows, only accessible on foot. In a part of the county known for its lavish fourteenth-century carving, this building is at the opposite end of the scale, with plain and simple architecture. The nave was originally three bays long with the bases of the southern piers widened to act as seats – hence the expression 'the weak go to the wall'. Then in the fifteenth century a tower was provided, but rather than add it onto the west end of the existing church, it was built inside the westernmost bay. If you stand in the vestry today, you can clearly see the half arch in the nave continuing under the tower and peering through the massive ashlar wall built to carry its weight. It might look clumsy, but it was a practical measure that meant they didn't have to worry about an added tower parting company from the older nave. At the beginning of the nineteenth century the medieval chancel was demolished and replaced by the patron, Robert Manners (d. 1828), grandson of the 2nd Duke of Rutland.

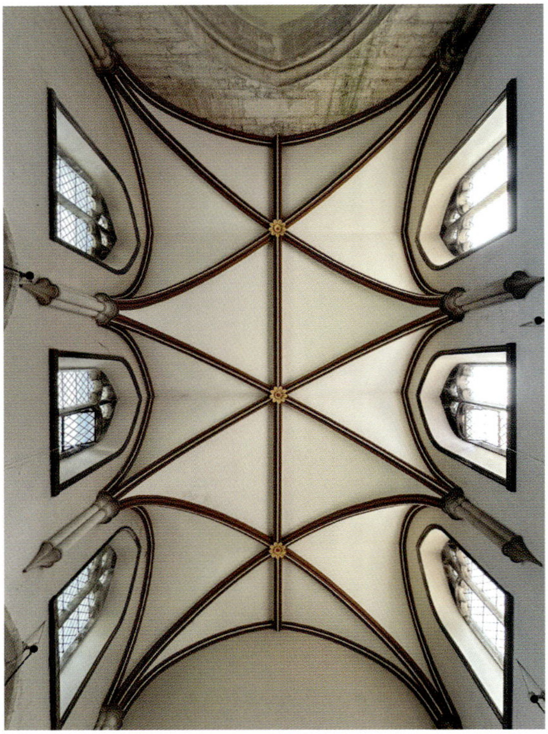

Left: Bloxholm. This unusual three-bay plaster vaulted ceiling dates from the alterations made to the church in 1812.

Below: Bloxholm. Over the main door is the shield of arms of General Manners, who beautified the church in 1812. It is made of artificial Coade stone which was cast in a mould – hence the fine detail.

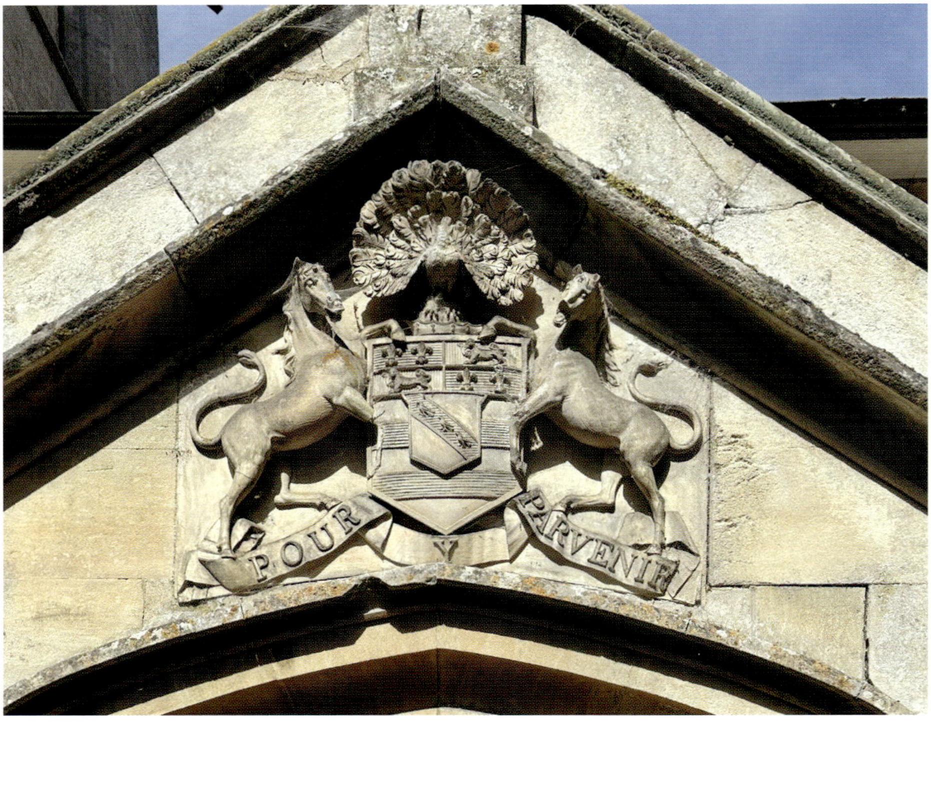

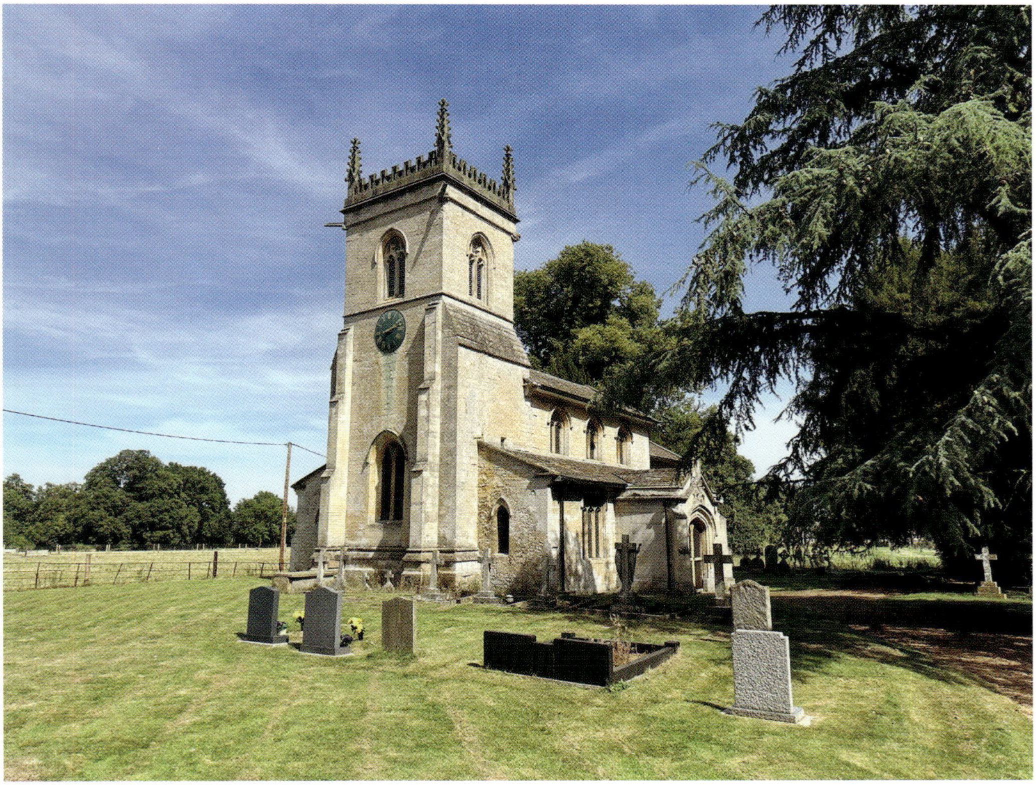

Bloxholm. Seen from the west, it is easy to see the use of smoothed stone, or ashlar, and the way in which the aisles clasp around the base of the tower.

He also paid for the simple vaulted ceiling in the nave and for the new porch which proudly displays his shield of arms and crest, which was a peacock. These arms are cast in artificial Coade stone and are signed Coade and Sealy, Lambeth, 1813. Robert's father, Lord Robert Manners (d. 1782), is buried under a ledger stone within the altar rails. The east window contains a small panel of enamelled glass depicting the Virgin and Child, of Continental manufacture. The churchyard boasts a fine selection of slate ledgers, many signed by their lettercutters with their place of manufacture displayed, including Ruskington, Sleaford and Heckington.

4. Boston, St Botolph

The tower of St Botolph's Church, popularly known as 'the Stump' is as iconic as Durham Cathedral or the Clifton Suspension Bridge. It is one of the best recognised buildings in England. Yet its completion in the early years of the sixteenth century came at a time when the once-prosperous port was no longer in good health, so the building was never completed. The putlog holes on the exterior of the tower, left when the wooden scaffolding that had been built into the structure was removed, remain unfilled to this day, giving the panelled corner buttresses the appearance

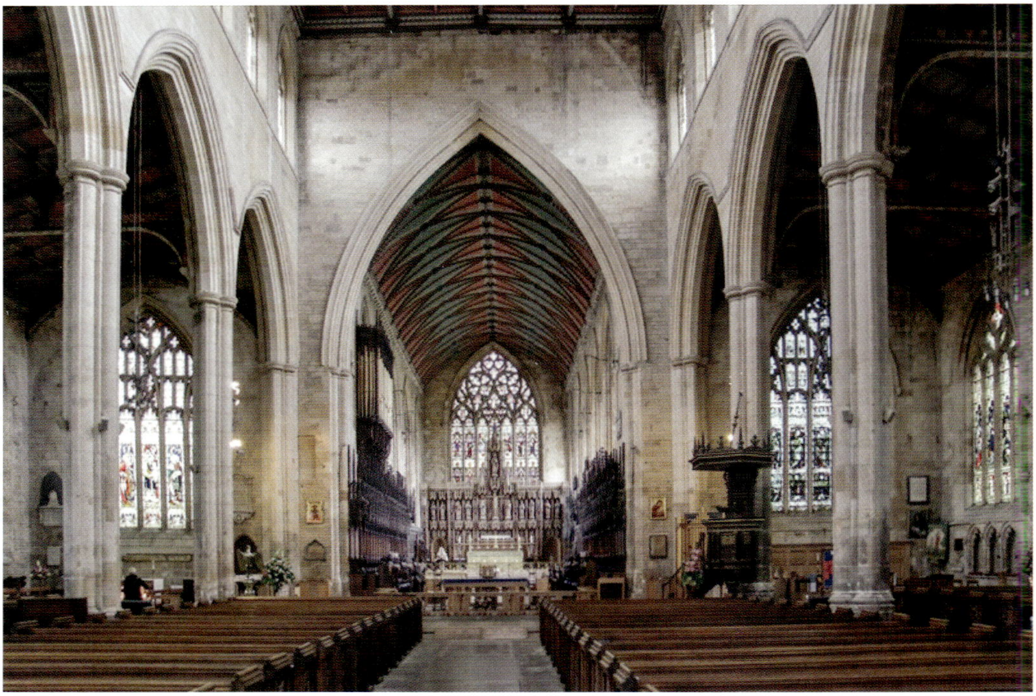

Boston. This stateliest of churches dates from the first half of the fourteenth century, just before the Black Death hit England.

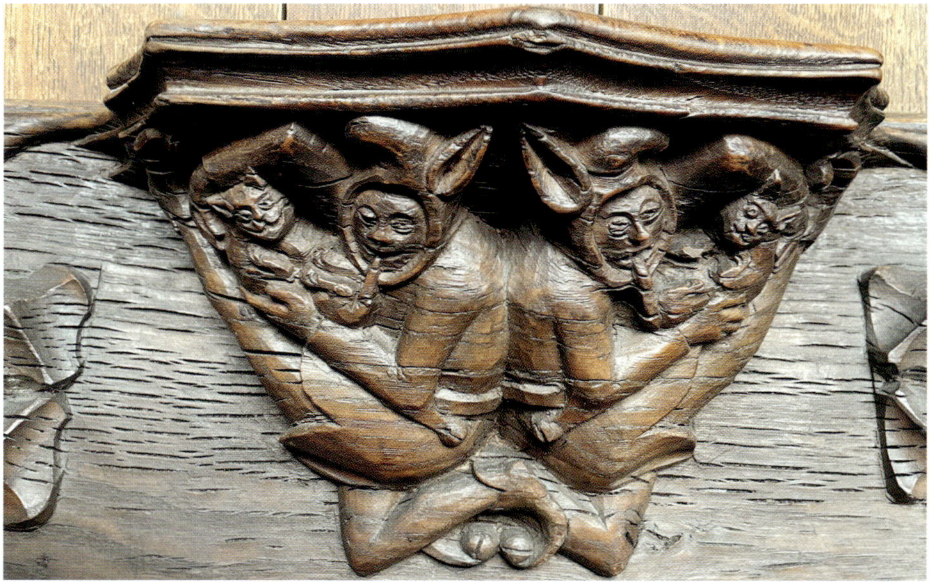

Boston. Amongst the fine set of misericords there are several humorous depictions, including this image of two jesters holding cats as if they were bagpipes and pretending to blow their tails. Were they suggesting that bagpipes sound like wailing cats?

of having been attacked by woodpeckers. The lantern on top of the tower was built both as a symbol of prestige, to the glory of God, and as a seamark. It must have once told seafarers that they were almost in the port. The church is entered by the original south door, built in the fourteenth century and covered in flowing wooden tracery. The room above the porch contains the church library. As may be expected, the church is large and light with almost the whole building visible at once. Surprisingly, the vaulting to the tower is nineteenth century, completing the unfinished work of 400 years earlier. The church contains much Victorian stained glass. The east window is by Irishman Michael O'Connor of 1853, an early study trying to recreate the feel of a medieval design. Any furnishings in a building of this size have to fight against the scale of the fabric, and the seventeenth-century gilded pulpit does not disappoint. In the chancel much is Victorian, including the reredos, which partly masks the east window, and the sedilia and canopies over the stalls. This was never a monastic church, and the stalls were purely a show of the enormous wealth of the town in the fourteenth century. Set within them are the stars of a visit to Boston: sixty-two misericords or tip-up seats, and it takes some time to view them all. The one that attracts a lot of attention is the schoolmaster meting out corporal punishment – medieval schoolmasters were often the local priest. Another 'joke' is the ape dressed as a monk examining a flask of urine. This was a dig at the perceived uselessness of the monastic life. However, my favourite depicts jesters playfully biting the tails of two cats.

5. Brant Broughton, St Helen

Almost every medieval church in the country was in a poor state of repair by the time Victorian piety and prosperity gave them the impetus to do something about the situation. In so many cases their enthusiasm to create a setting fit for purpose left us buildings which lack character and individuality, but here is a church where they enhanced and added to an already outstanding building. We know there was a Saxon church on the site from a surviving piece of sculpture, but as we see it today the building is of the Decorated period between 1250 and 1350. Although the whole church seems to be of a piece, only the western portion is original, the chancel having been rebuilt in the 1870s. The architects at this time were the firm of Bodley and Garner, who worked with the rector, Canon Sutton, a cultured and discerning man. The original nave was lavishly built; the north side being covered in carvings as it was the 'show front' facing the village. The south side is a little less elaborate, although both sides have majestic porches with vaulted ceilings and carvings underneath the eaves. Many are of foliate heads, or green men as they used to be called, representing the start of the story of the rood. On the south porch there is an exhibitionist figure, on his haunches and exposing his posterior – no doubt designed to scare away evil spirits. Inside, the perfectionism lavished on the church is clear to see. The structure of the nave is fourteenth century, but the Victorian decoration of the roof dominates; its design was based on the original. The aisles, too, have elaborately painted roof structures. The screen – complete with rood – frames the entrance to the more lavishly decorated chancel with a lierne vaulted ceiling painted in floral designs. The stained glass is unusual in

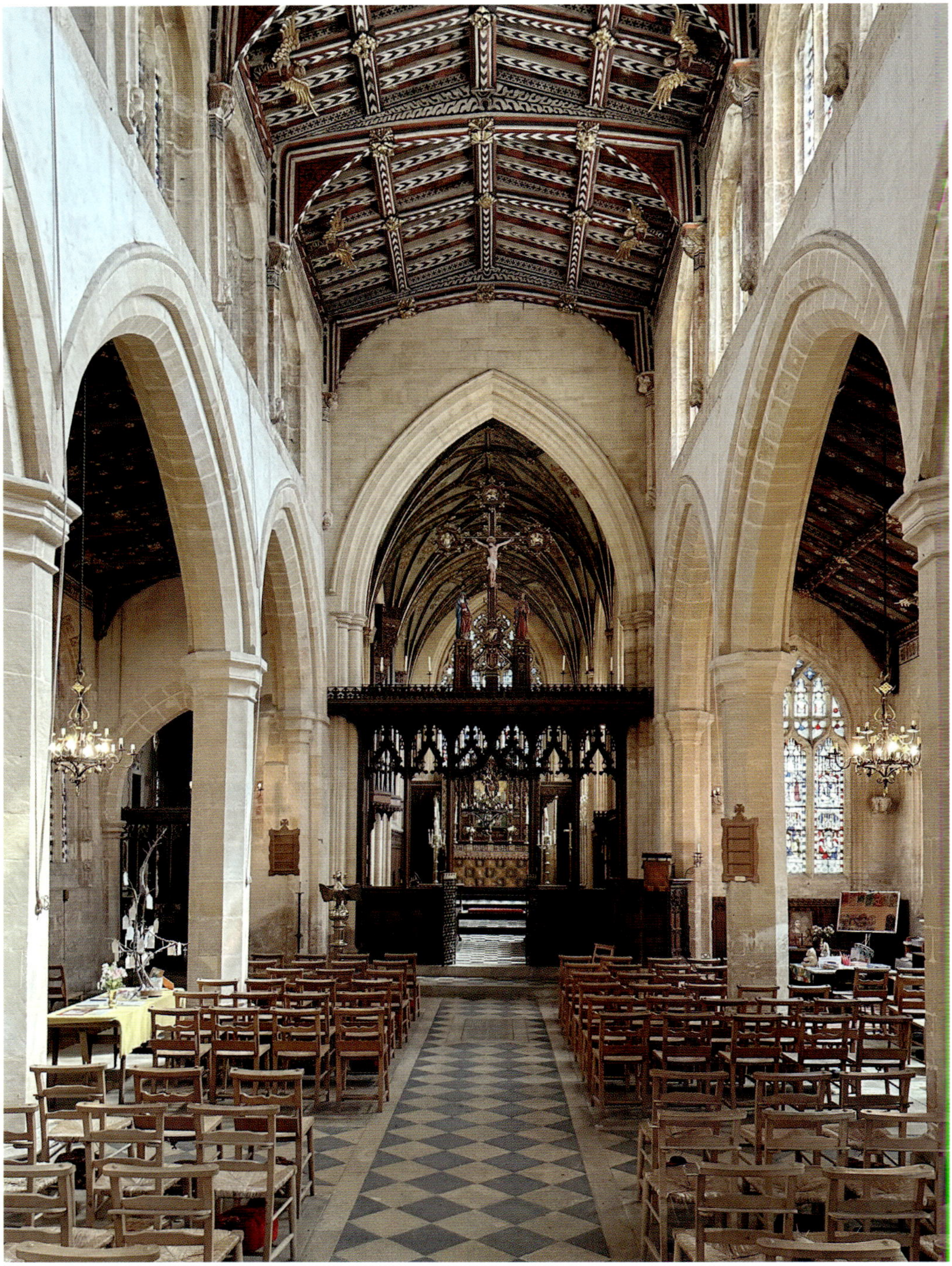

Brant Broughton. The character of the fourteenth-century interior is enhanced by the fittings added at the end of the nineteenth century to the designs of G. F. Bodley. The screen with its rood group helped return the interior to how it may have appeared when new.

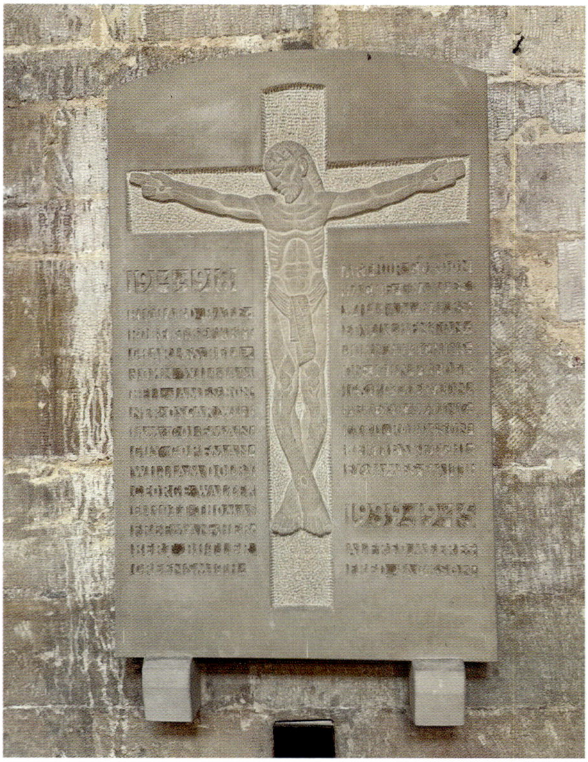

Brant Broughton. As well as its famous nineteenth-century furnishings, the church is also home to this striking war memorial by local sculptor Robert Kiddey whose work is of national importance.

that much of it was made by the rector in a kiln in his garden, although he had assistance from professionals, including Charles Kempe. Few rural churches present such an impressive interior and display what was possible when you had a cultured patron. Amongst the grandeur there are still earlier things to be found: at the back of the church is a fragment of a statue dating from the building of the church which shows the Trinity, and in the north chapel is a stone tomb chest that probably marks the grave of the original benefactor. As a reminder that churches are ever-evolving buildings, the wonderful war memorial tablet to commemorate those killed in the Second World War is by Robert Kiddey and shows that the best designs of each period can live in harmony.

6. Bratoft, St Peter and St Paul

In an area of large medieval churches. Bratoft comes as a surprise as it's a complete church in miniature. Most is of the familiar greenstone, although the tower is of local brick and dates from a rebuild of 1747. The odd 'double arch' visible inside proves that it replaced a medieval tower. The octagonal font carries the signs of the Passion and a foliate cat with plants issuing from its mouth. Whilst the church would originally have been limewashed and painted, this was removed post-Reformation, allowing us to see the use of limestone for the piers and greenstone blocks for the walls. Screens create chapels at the eastern ends

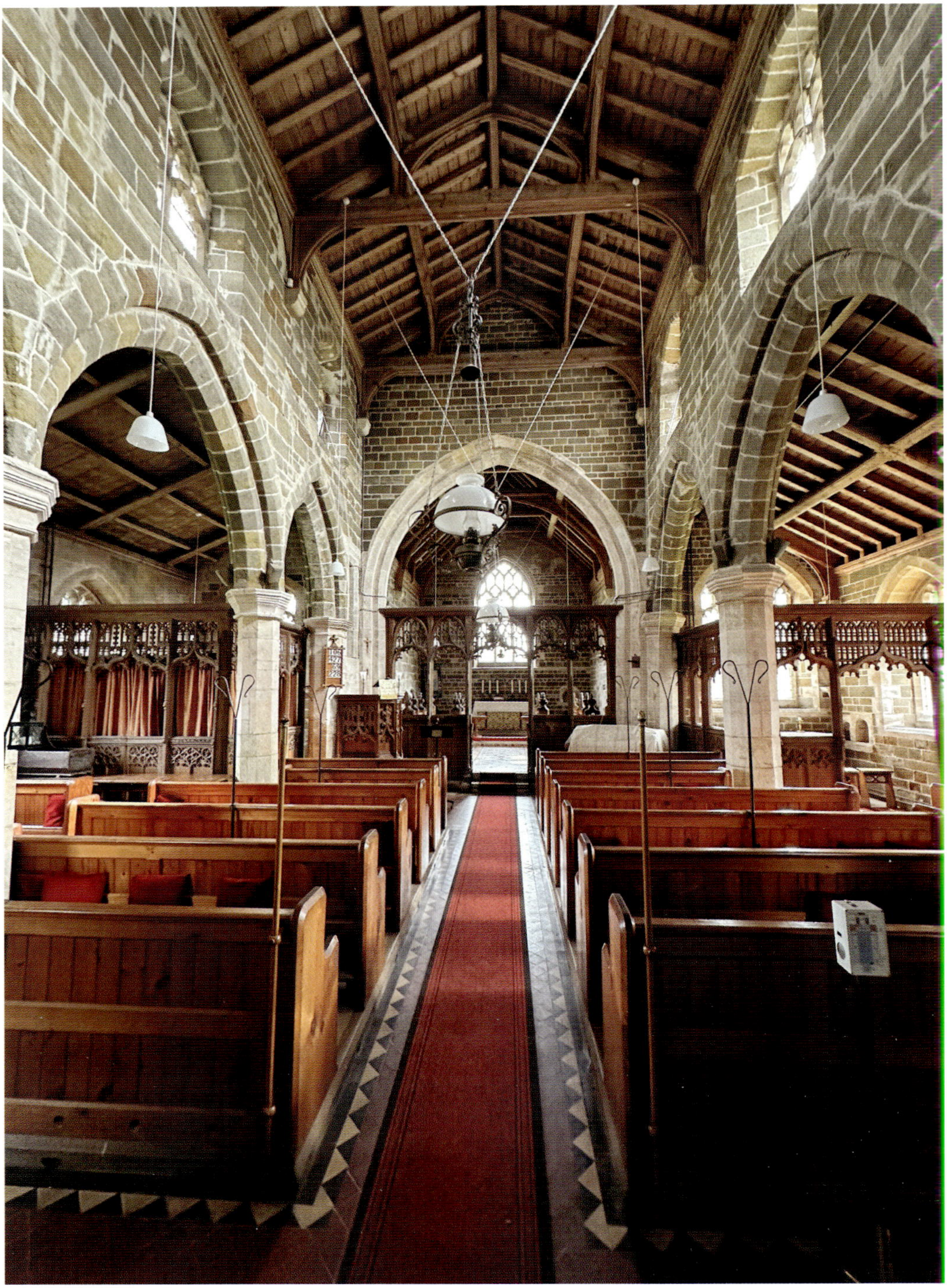

Bratoft. Interior looking east showing the scraped walls which give a very busy effect. Originally these walls would have been lime plastered.

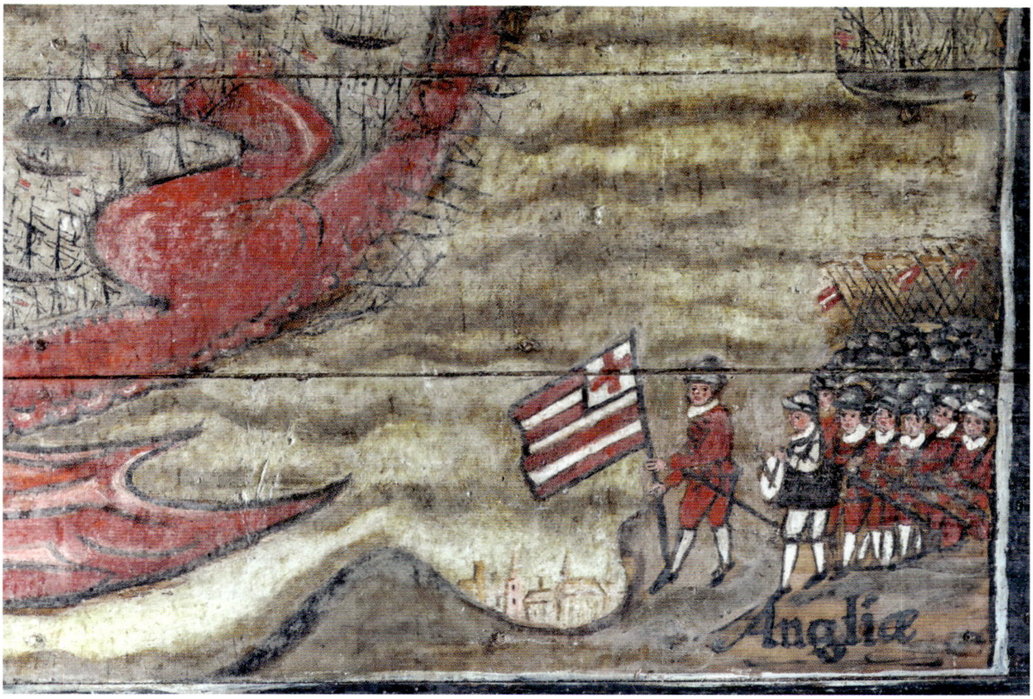

Bratoft. This unique painting depicts the Spanish Armada. Here we see the army waiting on English shores in case any Spanish ships land; however, they are encircled by a red dragon which represents a storm.

of both aisles, and there is a rood screen too, though almost all the woodwork is nineteenth century. Mounted on the wall is a 'Dead Man's Penny' awarded in memory of John William Scott, who was killed in the First World War. In order to appreciate the most important object in the church you'll need to walk down the nave and look back towards the tower; here, high on the wall, is a painting of the Spanish Armada off the south coast of England in 1588. There is a lot of artistic licence on display, especially in relation to the positioning of France, England, Scotland and Ireland, but the artist, Robert Stephenson, has certainly got the crescent formation of the Spanish ships correct. He has drawn a fierce red dragon around the Armada, which it is recorded in doggerel verse below returned just twenty-five ships to Spain. The religious conflicts of the sixteenth century had led to the Armada, by which means Spain hoped to reconvert the English to Catholicism. Someone in this parish was obviously keen to record its failure. Whilst it is signed, it lacks a date, but current opinion is that it is from the opening decades of the seventeenth century. The painting would originally have been within the tympanum of the chancel arch, and you can see that its left-hand side is still curved to fit. From the magnificent to the mundane: churches are often repositories of things that people no longer require, but quite how an eighteenth-century country cradle found its way into the north aisle is something of a mystery!

7. Brocklesby, All Saints

The church stands in the grounds of Brocklesby Hall, home of the Earl of Yarbrough, and public access is managed by the estate's office. The ironstone of which it is constructed is not hard wearing, so the exterior looks a little ragged, other than the eighteenth-century brick porch. Although the church consists of just nave and chancel, this is a building on a monumental scale only fully appreciated once you're inside. At the west end is a tremendous organ, the case of which came from the hall and was designed by the eighteenth-century architect James Wyatt. The nave is full of high-quality box pews and some window heads in the chancel retain fragments of fourteenth-century glass. A huge wooden eagle serves as a lectern and dates from the seventeenth century. But the monuments are what the visitor comes to see, dating from the Tudor period to the present day. On the north side of the chancel is Sir William Pelham (d. 1587), an alabaster monument with four male and four female effigies. His wife has a hand on a skull and one of her daughters holds one to show that they predeceased him. In the spandrels of the monument are the famous Pelham Buckles, part of the family heraldry. When William died he was severely in debt to the Crown. Opposite is the monument to his son, another William (d. 1629), who was left to repay his father's debts. It was commissioned from the London workshop of William Wright, who charged £100. William lies at a higher level than his wife, Ann Willoughby. Beneath is a crowd of children. Several hold skulls, but there are also three babies on the female side clothed in swaddling to show they died very young. There is some good heraldry

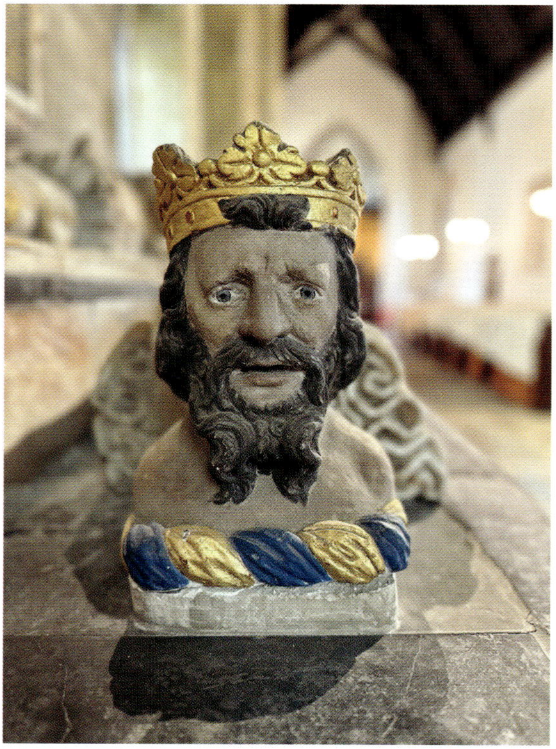

Brocklesby. The crest of the Willoughby family, a Saracen's head, sits proudly at the end of the monument to William Pelham and Ann Willougby.

here. At her feet is a Saracen's head ducally crowned, the Willoughby family crest, and at his head is a fine peacock which is the crest of the Pelhams. The chancel contains a battlefield cross from the First World War, originally on the grave of Lord Worsley, heir to the 4th Earl of Yarborough, who was killed in 1914. You can see the rotten base where it was sunk into the battlefield mud. Also displayed is the Dead Man's Penny presented to his family in remembrance of his service. At the west end of the nave is a window of 1963 commemorating the marriage at Cana.

8. Burgh le Marsh, St Peter and St Paul

The tall tower of this Perpendicular church can be seen for miles across the marshes, its clock proclaiming 'Watch and Pray for ye know not when the time is' bizarrely set with sun, moon and stars on a red background rather than blue which is more usual. The church contains some furnishings of exceptional quality. Firstly, the font of standard octagonal form has an impressive seventeenth-century cover in the classical form with open obelisks, which were such a feature of garden design at the time. The cover opens to allow the font to be used. Crowning the design is a more recent addition, a bird holding containers for ink and sand. It is the emblem of the Scrivener's Company, although a personal link has yet to be

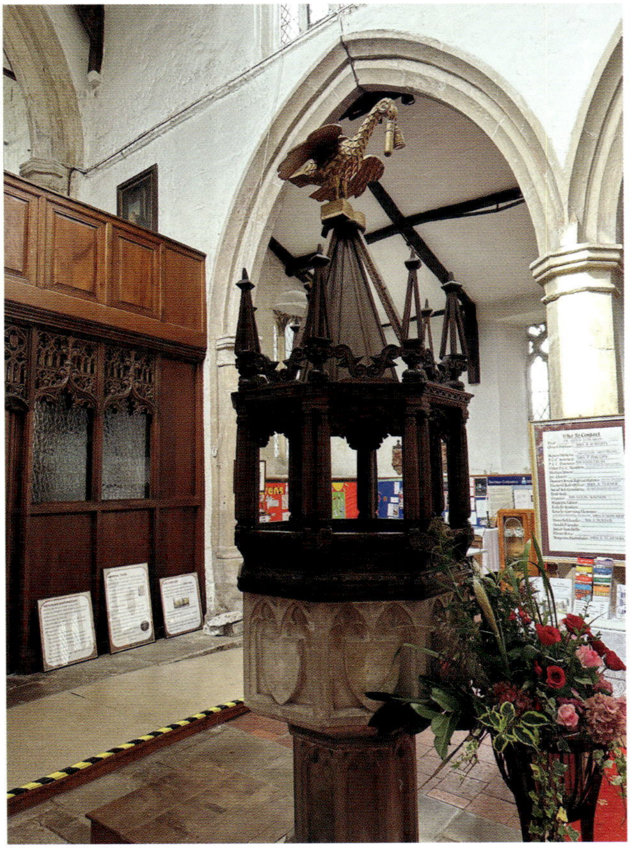

Burgh le Marsh.
The elaborate font cover with typical open obelisks dates from the seventeenth century. The extraordinary eagle on top is the emblem of the Scriveners Company, but when it was added to the cover and by whom is a complete mystery.

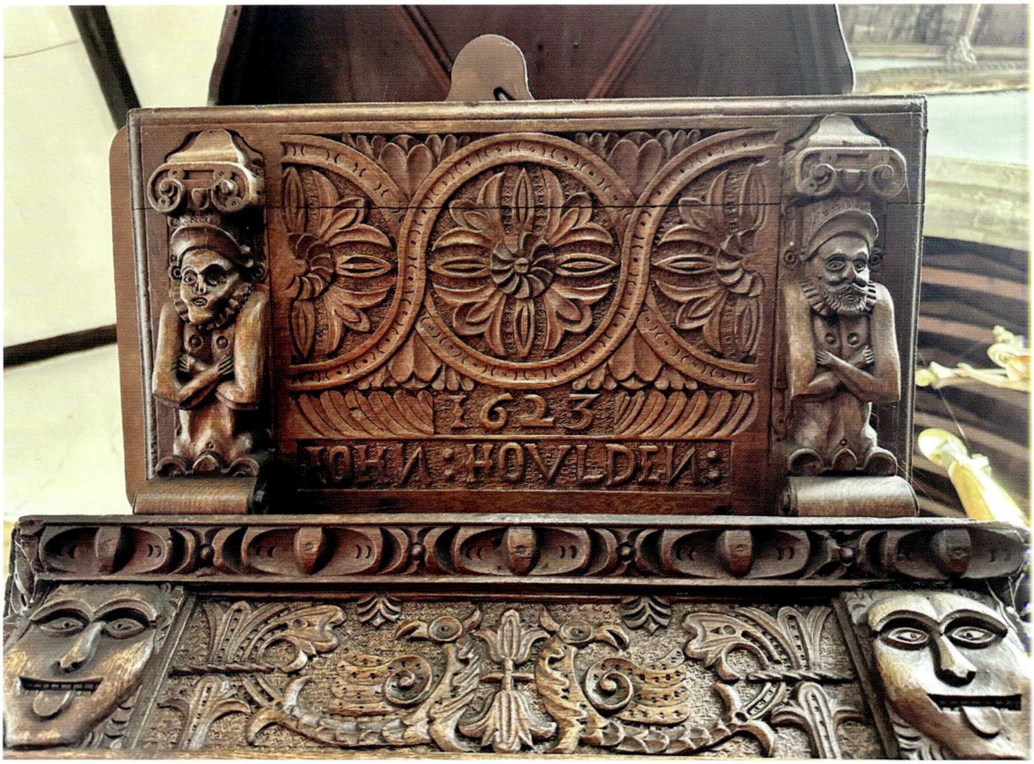

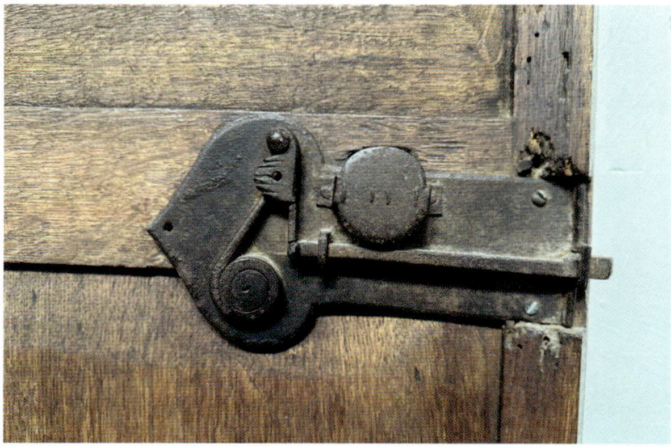

Above: Burgh le Marsh. Here we see the beautifully carved underside of the reading desk on the pulpit with the date 1623 and the name John Houlden. This is Jacobean workmanship of national importance.

Left: Burgh le Marsh. The sprung lock of the pulpit is a fine example of a local blacksmith's art and dates from the early seventeenth century.

established with anyone from the town. It formerly stood on the west gallery. Of the same date as the font cover is the screen in the south aisle, which rather cleverly avoids the fifteenth-century piers. It is likely to have formed a private pew, though now forms a side chapel. To the north of the chancel arch, the pulpit is of the same construction. This is dated underneath the bookrest 1623 and shows the name John Shoulden, who may have been the carver, incumbent or churchwarden. Don't get distracted by the topless grotesques – the carver certainly had fun! The pulpit is of wineglass shape with a richly carved back panel depicting the royal arms and a tester supported by an iron bracket. In fact, it doesn't have a plain surface on show. Only the inside is plain, and it is here that you can find the original catch carefully made by the village blacksmith, set on a heart-shaped backplate. It is these little details that make original furniture so appealing. Opposite the pulpit is the fearsome wooden lectern. Rather than the usual graceful eagle of St John the Evangelist, here we have a real bruiser carved by Victorian village hairdresser and eccentric Jabez Good. The roof is supported on stone brackets, several of which are carved. One is especially interesting (take binoculars) as it shows a baby bird being plucked by its parent from the mouth of a boggle-eyed monster. In a church with few monuments, a brass inscription to Leonard Palmer (d. 1610) is a list of questions and answers, the last being 'Ubi mens est defuncti: Rogitas dubio procul astra petivit'. (Do you enquire where the soul of the deceased is? Doubtless it has sought the stars.)

9. Burton upon Stather, St Andrew

The churches of north Lincolnshire are generally less well known than their southern counterparts, but several offer rich pickings. St Andrew's is situated on high ground looking west to the River Trent, near its confluence with the Humber. The church doesn't seem very promising from the outside, but inside its architectural interest is in the north arcade. This presents something of a conundrum because all the details are of the late Romanesque period, whilst the arches are pointed. It may be that they were originally round headed and have been reassembled, or that they represent a strange hybrid in what used to be known as a transitional form. The carving is very crisp and the chain-like carvings on the central arch are especially prominent. It will be seen that the piers supporting them are of different designs, indicating that the arcade took a long time to complete under the patronage of Runcorn Priory, to whom the church was granted in 1115. The south arcade is late thirteenth century and was part of a rebuilding scheme which heightened the walls and installed the clerestory windows. At the west end of the south aisle the stained-glass window of Christ which dates from the Georgian period may have come from elsewhere as part of it is in another window nearby. Further along is a stunning window of 1986 designed by Tony Hollaway, whose best-known works are in Manchester Cathedral. It is an abstract design depicting the motion of water, sea, sun and moon. Since 1589 the church has been in the patronage of the Sheffield family of Normanby, so the chancel contains their monuments. Outstanding amongst them is the disconsolate lady leaning against an urn which is to Sir Charles Sheffield, 1st Baronet (d. 1774). He was the illegitimate son of the 1st Duke of Buckingham and Normanby and is best known as the man who sold Buckingham House to King George III in 1761. The sculptor was John Fisher the Elder of York, one of the finest craftsmen of his day. Opposite is the modest plaque by Thomas Gaffin of London to the 3rd Baronet's widow, Sarah Ann, which pictures two sheaves of cut corn. The extraordinary plaster angels springing from the corbels of the chancel roof are particularly impressive and date from a restoration of 1886 in memory of the 5th Baronet.

10. Burwell, St Michael

It is said that St Michael first appeared in AD 490 at Monte Gargano in Italy, and ever since has been associated with high places. It's certainly true that many hilltop churches bear his dedication, and Burwell is no exception. There is no vehicular access to the church, which is reached by a footpath from the main road. The first thing the visitor sees is an enormous rabbit warren under the ancient yew trees. They love digging through centuries-old graves, and disarticulated bones are often to be seen. Externally, the church shows that it was originally much larger, with four blocked arches that would have led into a south aisle. The brick top of the tower is a repair of the eighteenth century, strengthened from the beginning by iron X braces. Inside, the church is tall and light. Look up inside the tower to see some large medieval wooden angels, saved when the nave roof was rebuilt. The font bears an inscription around the base which tells us that it was the gift of Thomas Fitzwilliam in 1468, and no doubt his shield of arms would have been painted on the (now blank) shields around the bowl. There is an unusual bronze First World War memorial on the north wall which records the names of four men who did not return. A little further down the nave we can appreciate the twelfth-century chancel arch which has a crudely carved capital on the north side depicting two horses; the pulpit gives us easy access to see it close up. High above the pulpit is an important fragment of wall painting depicting a crowned woman.

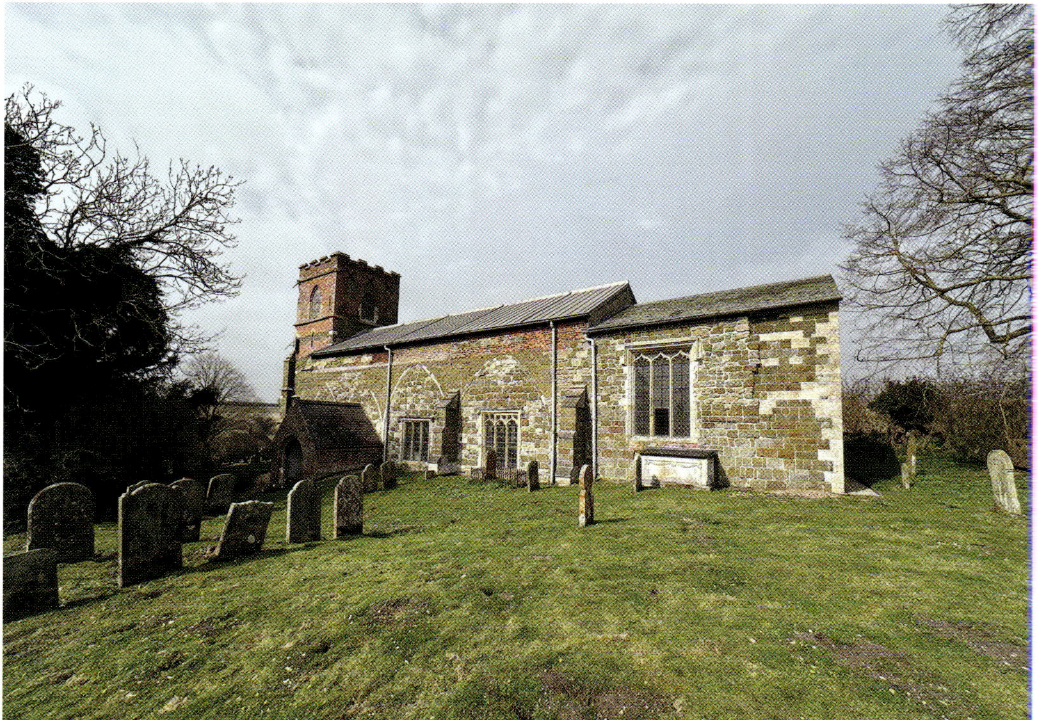

Burwell. High on its hill above the village sheltered in the valley. The four blocked arches once led to a south aisle.

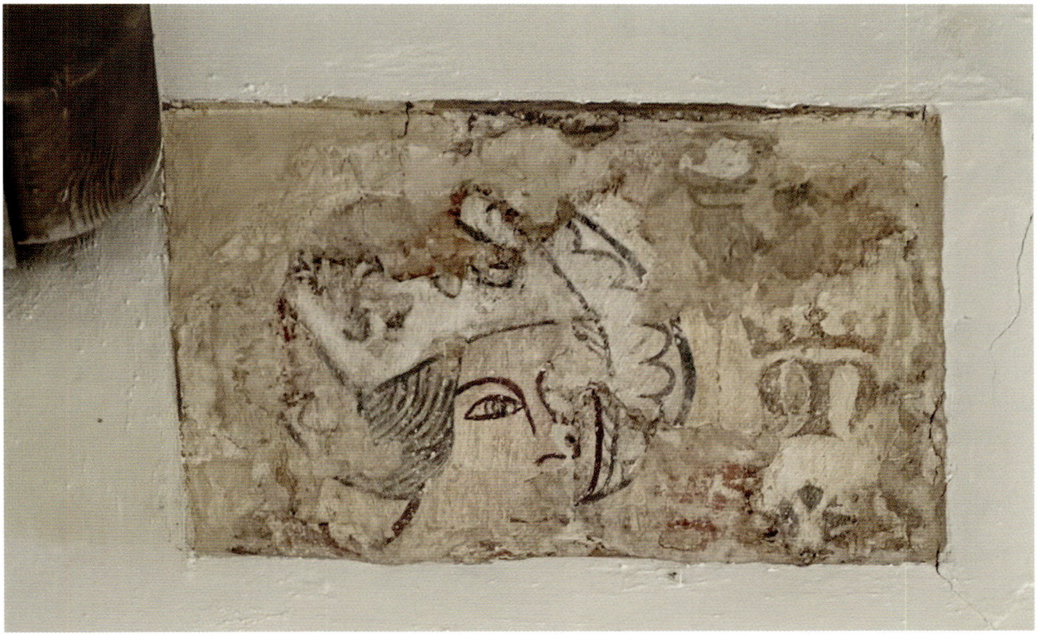

Above: Burwell. This tiny fragment of medieval wall painting depicts a queen with a halo, so is possibly Our Lady as Queen of Heaven.

Right: Burwell. Missed by many, this is the underside of an image bracket that once supported a statue. Traces of its original paint survive.

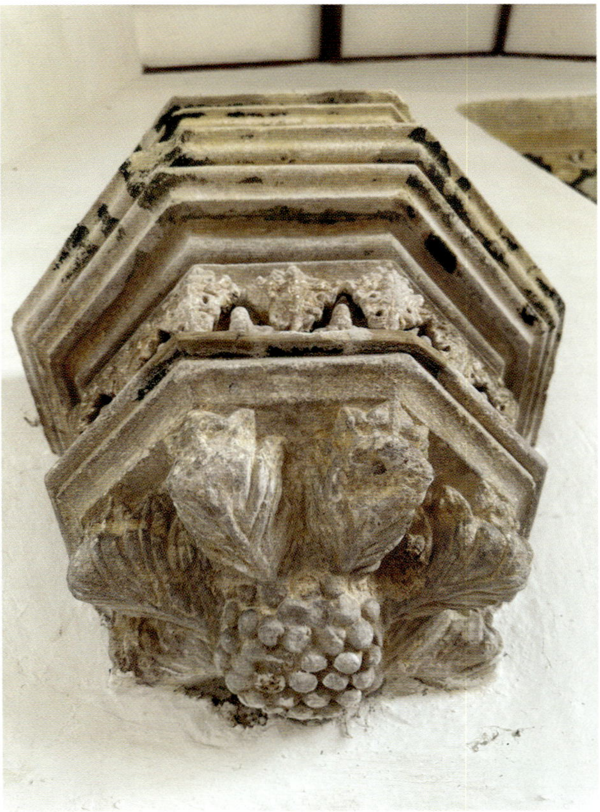

Just to her right is a crowned 'M', which is usually associated with Our Lady, so this probably represents her as Queen of Heaven. Immediately under the step is a stone inscribed 'Entrance' which gives access to the Yorke vault underneath the chancel. One half of a heavily carved altar rails depicting bunches of grapes dating from 1910 survives and matches the wooden altar gifted in 1915, which has a stone Mensa or top with its traditional five crosses incised. Above the altar is the most important object in the church: a fifteenth-century image bracket, deeply carved with acanthus leaves under a quatrefoil frieze. Traces of its red and green paint survive. Nearby is a tablet commemorating Robert Christison (d. 1915) a pioneer settler in Australia, who developed huge sheep farms there and experimented with the embryonic frozen meat trade. His inscription tellingly records that he 'entered a wider sphere'.

11. Burton Coggles, St Thomas Becket

The treasures of this church are two early fourteenth-century effigies in the porch. As you step in to see them, look at your feet; you are stepping on a thirteenth-century stone coffin lid. We do not know who these knights were, but the one on the east side is particularly well carved with chain mail and the other lies with a canopy at his head. It is a miracle that they were preserved when the church was restored rather than being consigned to the churchyard. The restoration of 1873 was by Edward Welby Pugin, son of the famous A. W. Pugin. The west wall of the nave tells a good story, for high up we can see a Norman window which now leads

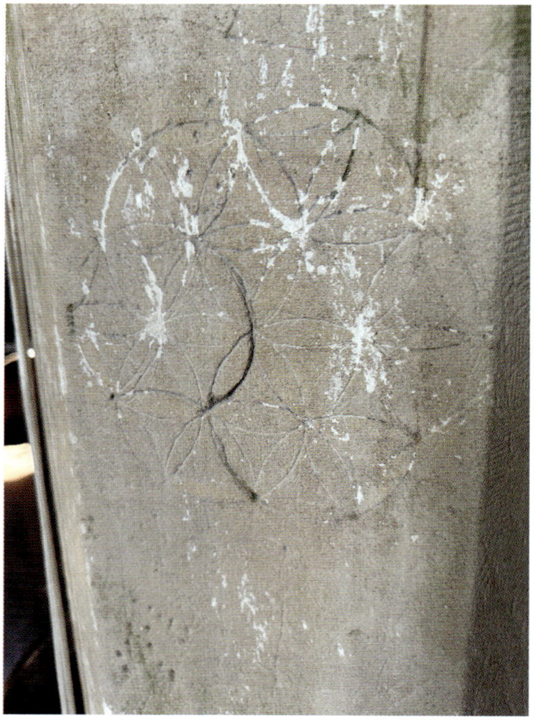

Burton Coggles. This medieval graffiti takes the form of 'witch marks'. These were supposed to catch evil spirits who, once they got into the circles, were unable to get out.

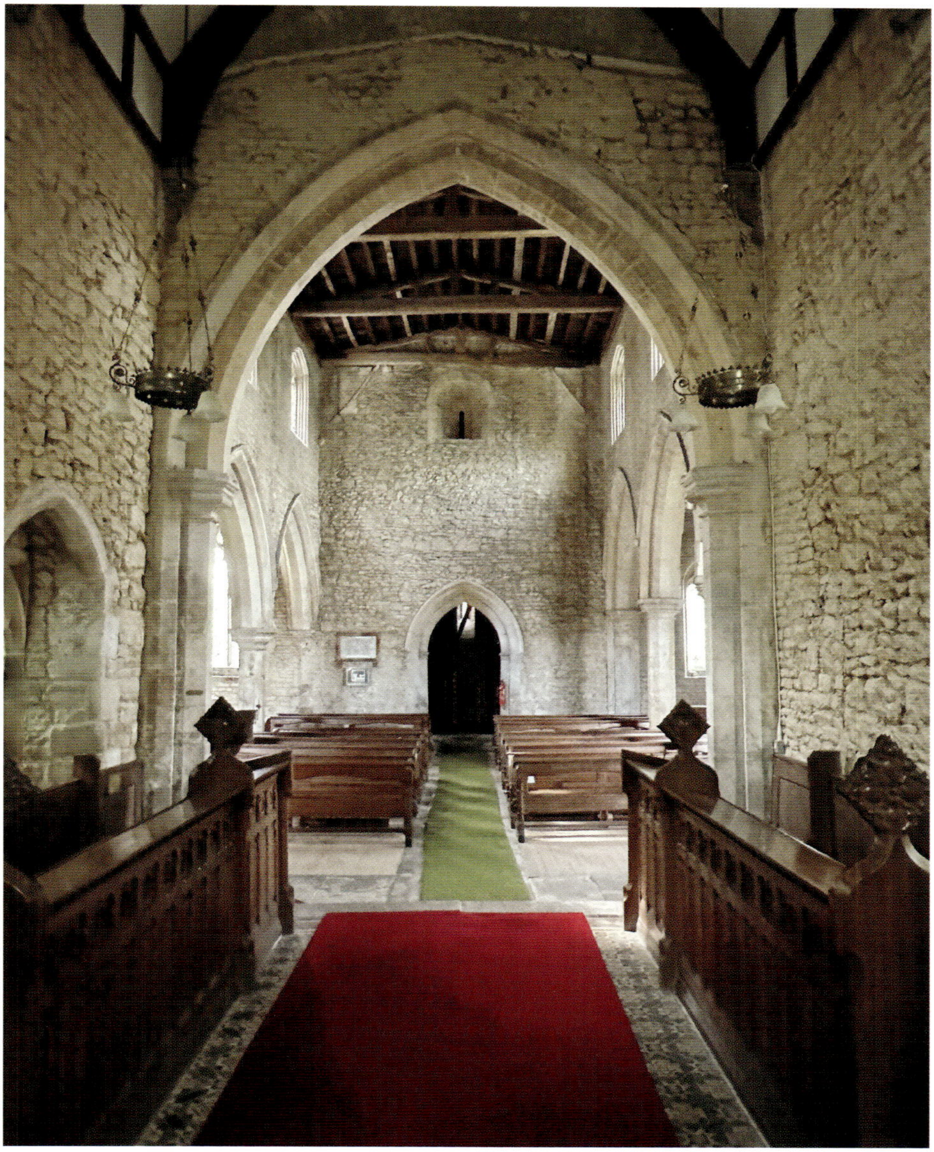

Burton Coggles. Interior looking west. You can clearly see the original Norman window which now looks into the later tower. The outline of the original roof may be seen before the walls were raised to insert the clerestory windows.

into the tower, whilst above it is the scar of a previous roof. This tells us that the walls of the nave must be Norman and that the tower and the aisles were added in the late 1200s. It is also just possible to pick out some horizontal changes in the stonework, each of which relates to a different campaign of building in the twelfth century. On the east pier of the north aisle is a large group of 'daisy wheel' graffiti. These were apotropaic symbols designed to 'catch' evil spirits. There are several thirteenth-century piscinae in the church, the most interesting being in the south aisle where at a later date it was converted into an aumbry – or cupboard – as evidenced by the surviving hinges. In the chancel is an unusual sedilia. Rather than being formed of carved arches, it is created in the East Anglian way by dropping the windowsill to make a seat for the priest at Mass. It is now outside the altar rails, but the latter were post-Reformation additions so the seats would originally have formed part of the furnishings of the altar. There is also a low side window to give ventilation during the Mass and to cause the lamps on the rood screen to flicker. High in the roof of the south aisle are two wooden carvings of musicians each playing a wind instrument.

12. Caythorpe, St Vincent

There are two things the visitor will remember from this delightful church. Firstly, the stripey exterior built in alternate layers of ironstone and limestone which gives an unusual effect. Most rubble-built churches were designed to be lime rendered externally, but this cannot have been the case here where so much effort went into the design. Secondly, the church is one of a handful in England to have an arcade running down the centre of the nave. Consequently, it is not the easiest of buildings to use, but the addition of a north aisle by Sir Gilbert Scott in 1860 helped make things slightly easier. Quite why the original church had an arcade running into the centre of the chancel arch is unclear. It may have been

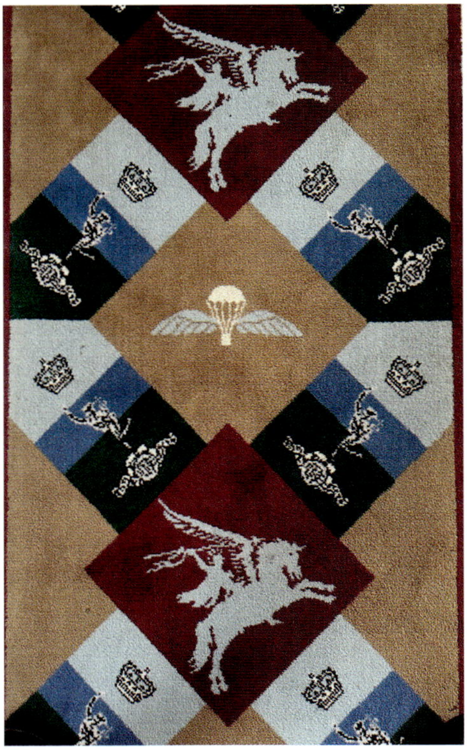

Caythorpe. This carpet reminds us of the links between the church and 216 (Parachute) Signal Squadron.

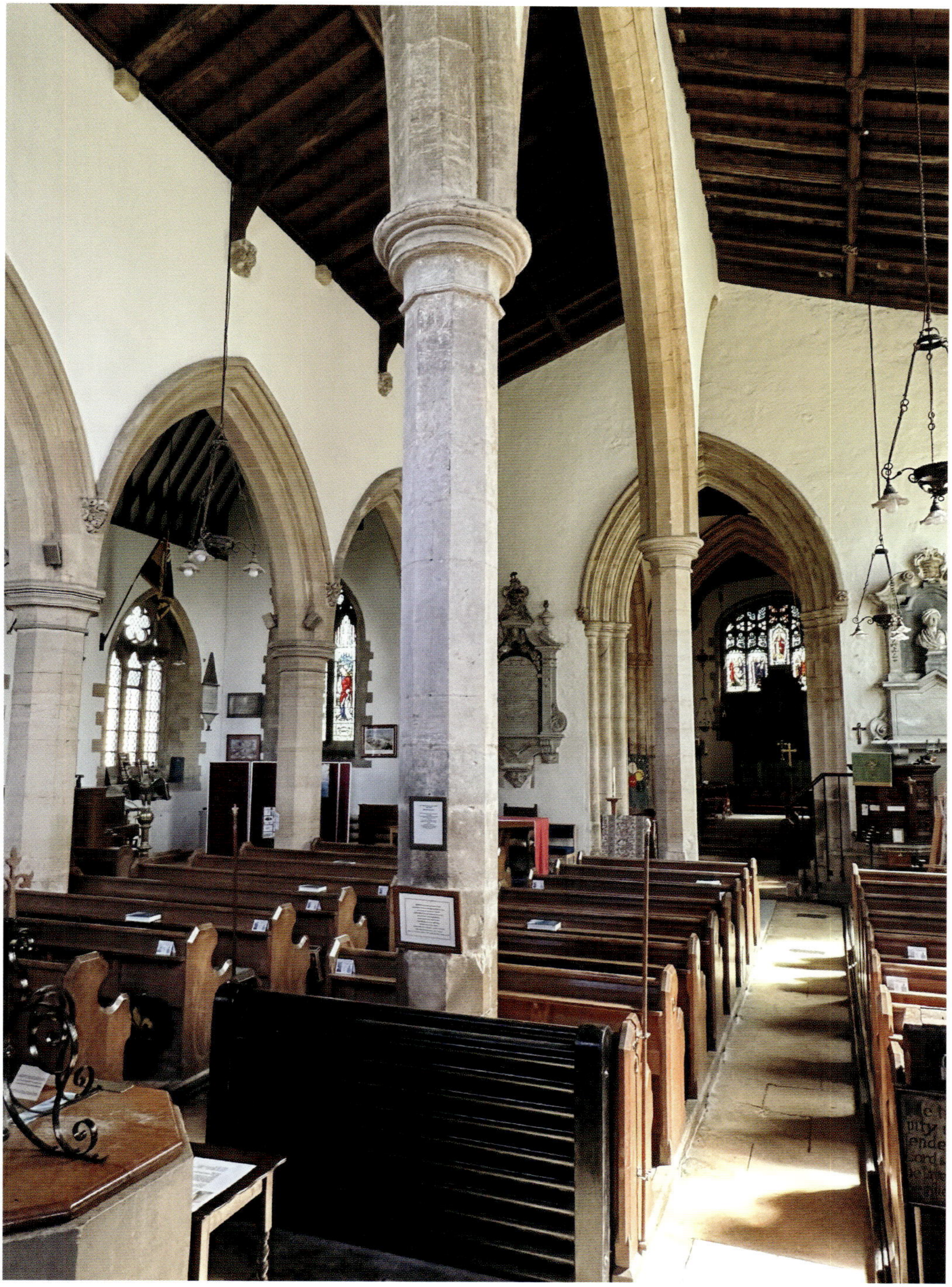

Caythorpe. The bizarre interior was created when the nave was originally built and is not the result of later alterations. Perhaps the builders were unsure as to their abilities.

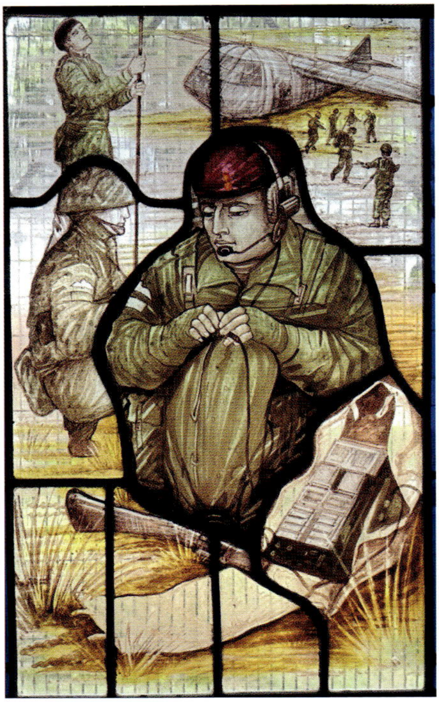

Caythorpe. Stained glass in what is now called the 'Arnhem aisle' depicts many aspects of military life.

apprehension on the part of the builders who worried that their roof might not be properly supported. A walk around the outside is recommended because there is a rare surviving medieval carving of the Annunciation on a buttress, a Mass dial on the porch and on the south wall of the nave two blocked low side windows, which must have given light onto a nave altar. The porch still retains its stone benches for witnesses at weddings and legal ceremonies which all took place here in the medieval period. The tower crossing stands between the nave and chancel and it is here that you can find all sorts of mason's marks and graffiti scratchings. Now brought inside, there is a charming inscription on a headstone in the chancel to Edmund Weaver (d. 1748), who is described as 'one of the best astronomers of his age'. By the door is a poor box with three locks and a quotation from Proverbs. The north aisle is now known as the 'Arnhem Aisle' and maintains a link with 216 (Parachute) Signal Squadron. Two stained-glass windows show military scenes, and a lovely carpet is stitched with the symbols of the Parachute Regiment and the Royal Signals.

13. Claypole, St Peter

This atmospheric church is entered via a wicket door in the porch, crudely cut into the larger fourteenth-century structure. It leads into a light interior where it is immediately obvious that the capitals in the nave are of higher than usual quality. They take the form of foliate designs and, unusually for a parish church, the carving is undercut to provide a 3D effect. There are transepts leading off

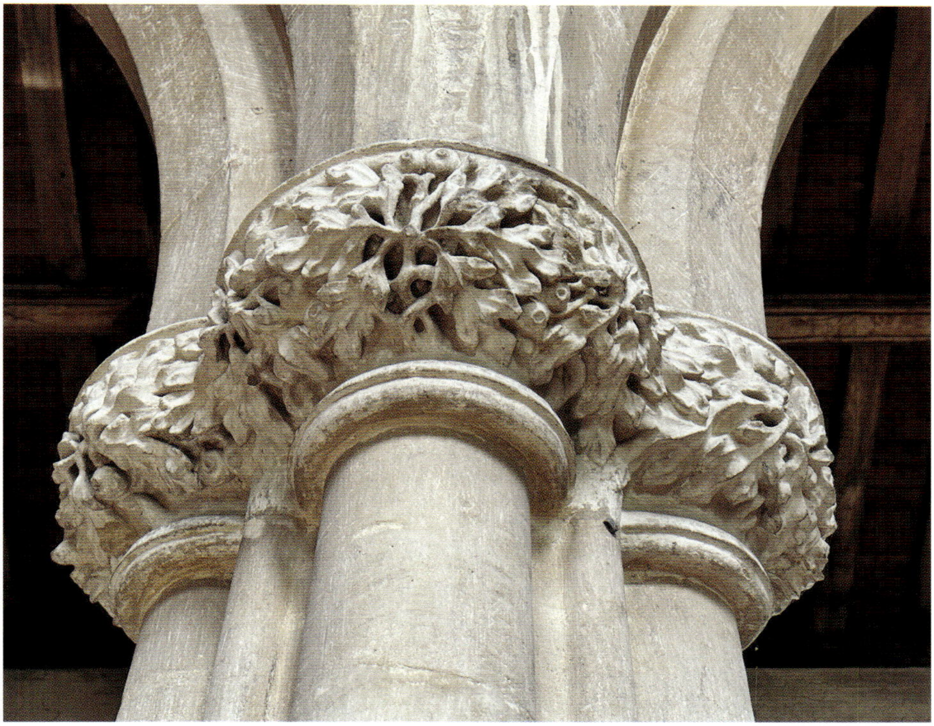

Claypole. The foliate capitals are of extremely high quality and date from the second half of the fifteenth century.

the nave and because they are of unequal shape it has been suggested that the southernmost is an older freestanding chapel that was later incorporated into the building. This would explain the set of sedilia in the transept, where the clergy at Mass used to sit, and which are usually only found in the chancel. The double piscina here (the drains for the priest to wash the vessels and his fingers) helps us date this group to about 1300. The east end hoodmoulds of the transeptual arches are cut away to allow for the rood, which crossed the arch above the surviving medieval screen. Above this on both sides is a pair of high windows, the light from which would have fallen on the rood figures themselves. In front of the screen is a medieval wineglass pulpit, its later sounding board made up of medieval carved fragments. The chancel contains much of interest and the sedilia here are much more elaborate than those in the transept and are a little later, dating from the fourteenth century. We are helped in knowing more about them as the canopy includes the shields of arms of the donors – the Cressy, Simeon and Hebden families. On the right-hand edge of the sedilia is a rare thing indeed: a metal hook in the wall which once held one end of the Lenten veil, which shielded the high altar from view during Lent. Sadly, its counterpart on the north side has long since disappeared. There is a highly decorated aumbry opposite the sedilia, designed as part of the set. This is where the sacred vessels would have been stored. If you turn around at the altar and look west you can see a glorious example of

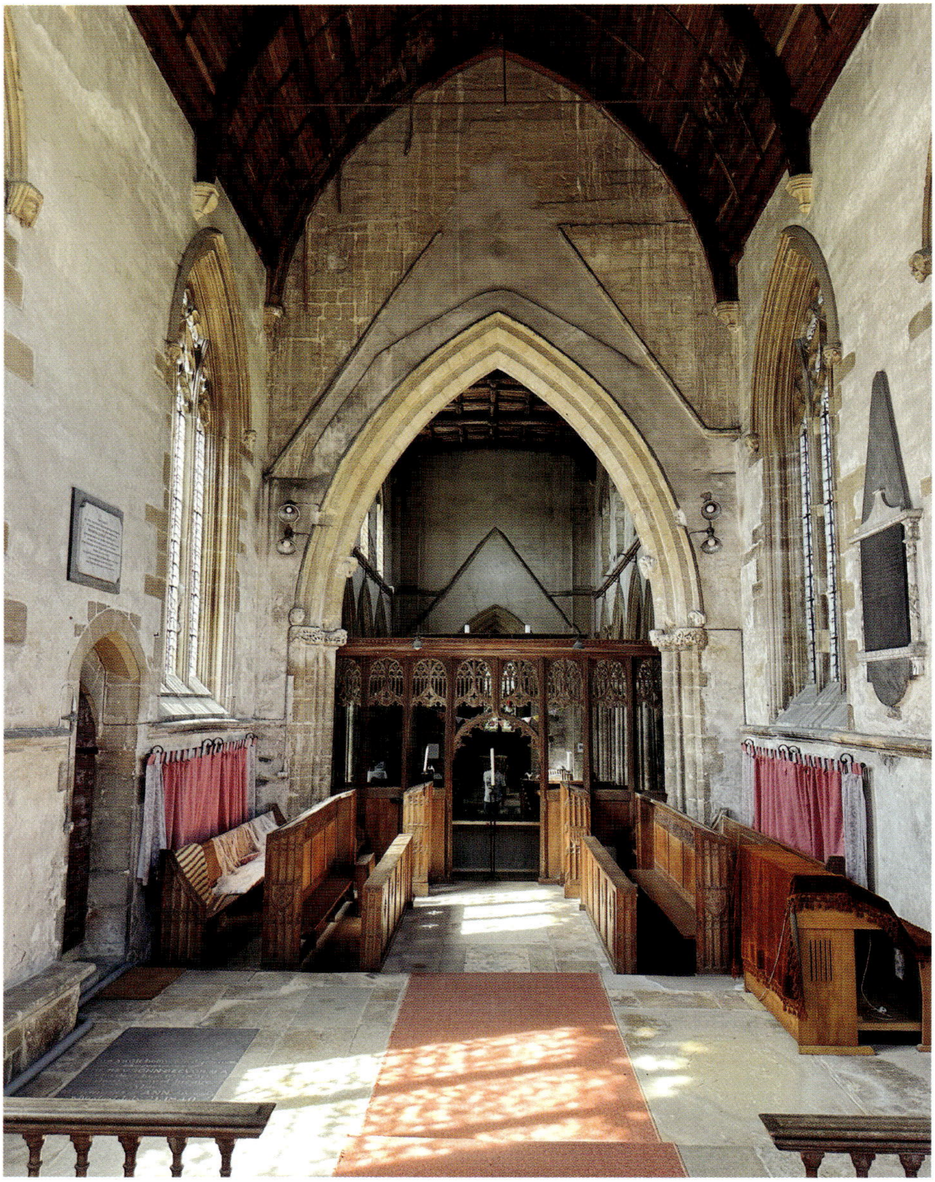

Claypole. Interior looking from the large chancel towards the west where several early roof lines may be seen. The new nave roof gave room for clerestory windows which was a practical benefit, but the chancel roof was rebuilt to give a more impressive setting for Mass.

'vertical archaeology', where the former roof lines of the earlier chancel and nave can be clearly seen as scars below the present. The church has little stained glass, but I always have to smile when I see the twentieth-century window depicting St Nicholas, St Peter and St Hugh of Lincoln, each of whom looks as if he doesn't want to be there!

14. Coates, St Edith

This diminutive Norman church punches well above its weight in atmosphere and interest. Standing in a sequestered churchyard set within a working farm, it is the epitome of the English country church. Built of limestone rubble, the architectural distinction between nave and chancel is almost invisible. On the south side a tiny twin-opening window carved from a single piece of stone marks the position of the rood loft staircase inside; the south door displays a fine series of dogtooth mouldings, although they seem rather too crisp to be true. Perhaps they were recut by the Victorians? Inside the church other nineteenth-century repairs are hardly noticeable, such is the plethora of surviving medieval work. At the junction of nave and chancel, in place of a stone arch, is a five-bay wooden screen which retains its rood loft. Moreover, above it is a wooden tympanum which retains traces of medieval decoration from the rood, including the face of Our Lady. Even higher up, on the roof timbers, there are the remains of carved decoration which would have provided a canopy, or celure, over the statue of the crucified Christ. From the patina of the timber, it is easy for the visitor to see what is original work and what is an 1883 replacement. The doorway to the stairs – whose window we saw outside – is on the south side and retains its original wooden frame. The church has eight rustic benches, whilst a Jacobean family pew with gorgeous S hinges sits just inside the chancel. The plain tub font is Norman, though suffering from rising damp, whilst above it hangs a seventeenth-century royal arms, the painted decoration now sadly almost gone. There are some fine monuments. On the north wall of the nave is a cusped arched recess, possibly built together with the

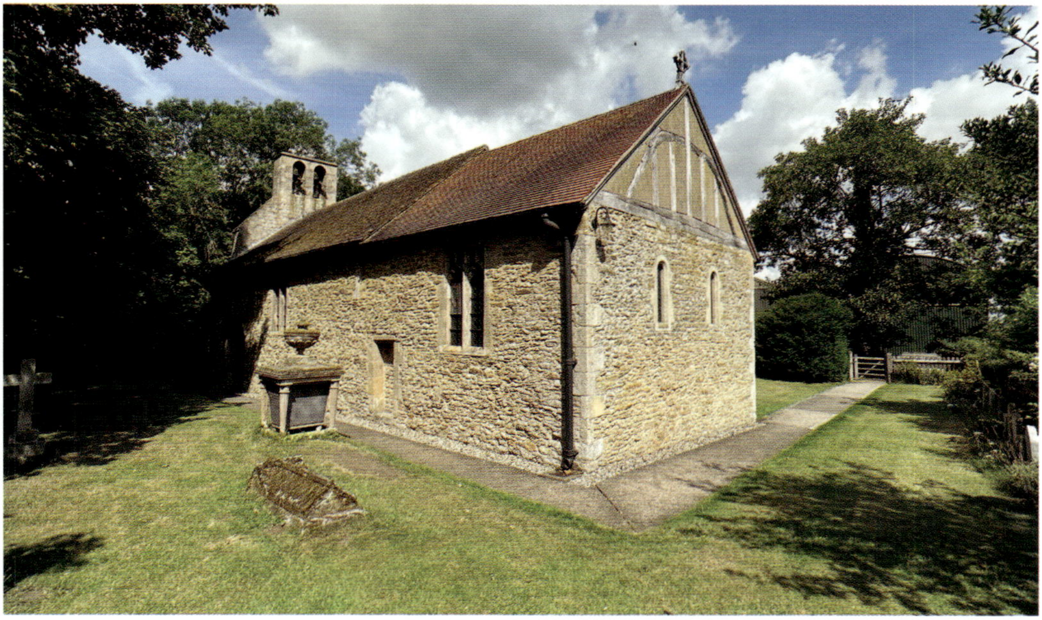

Coates. An unassuming church in a farmyard setting with two Norman windows and a door surviving from its earliest build. The tomb with the urn is unusual in being signed by its sculptor, Richard Chamberlain of Newark, 1825.

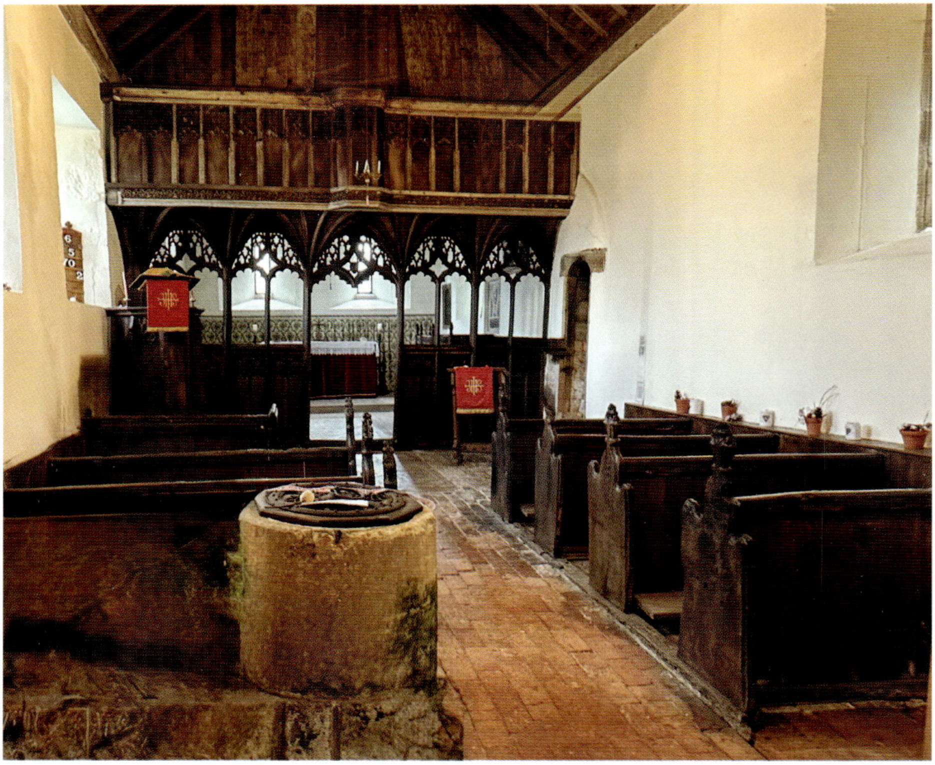

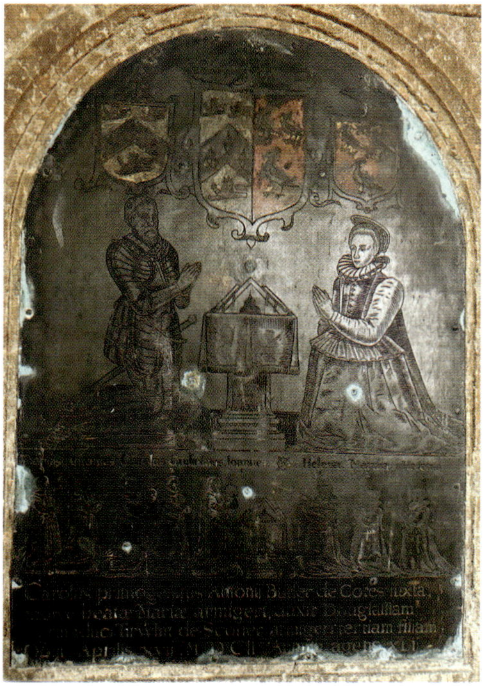

Above: Coates. Interior looking east, with the tub font of Norman period. The screen and infilled tympanum above are medieval and it is just possible to pick out traces of paint on the latter.

Left: Coates. Brass inscription to Charles Butler (d. 1602), his wife and eight children who are named separately.

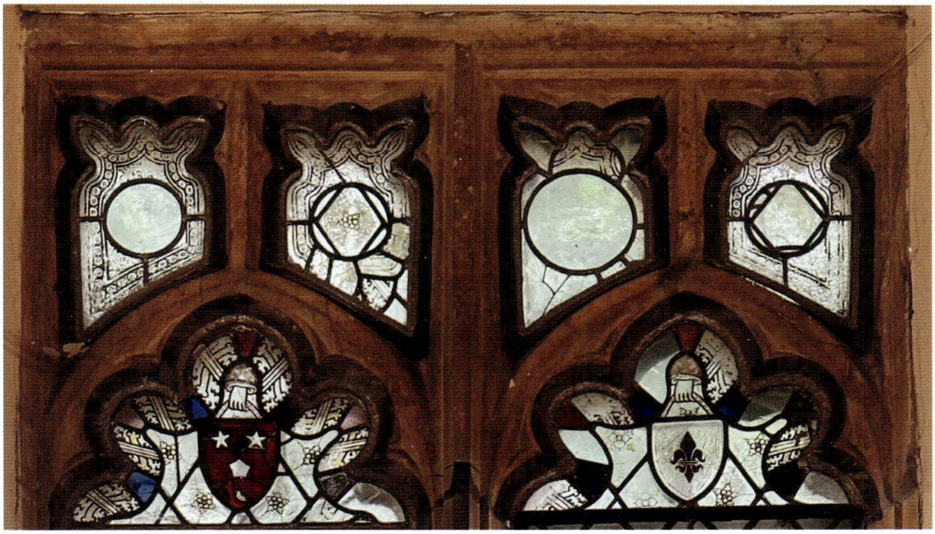

Coates. Surviving medieval glass depicting two shields of arms which are suspended by ghostly hands.

large window above it in the fifteenth century. In the chancel an alabaster wall monument depicts the rather portly Brian Cooke (d. 1653), whilst several brass plates recall members of the Butler family. That of 1590 to William Butler is in the medieval tradition of cut-out brass figures, including a dead baby, her head on a pillow, whilst the others are in the contemporary tradition of using a single piece of metal inscribed as a picture. The brass to Charles Butler (d. 1602) still retains some colour in its heraldry and shows five sons and three daughters beneath. Three children are holding skulls to show that they predeceased their father. There are fragments of heraldic glass in the church – I especially like the heraldic tracery which shows the shields of arms being displayed on ropes held by tiny hands.

15. Crowle, St Oswald

On the border with Yorkshire and not far from the M62, the small town of Crowle boasts an interesting church which houses a superb example of pre-Conquest art. As you approach from the south, past a medieval preaching cross, it is easy to see its Norman origins as the south wall of the nave is divided horizontally by a corbel table, or row of small carved heads. These would originally have been at the top of the first wall, just underneath the eaves, but the walls were later heightened. Despite much weathering an array of animals may be seen. The church is entered through a massive Norman doorway and you step down into the church, the difference in floor level indicating the rise in the ground level of the churchyard over a millennium. The interior has been much altered. The north aisle was originally added in the thirteenth century, was later demolished, and rebuilt by the Victorians. In the south wall are two early stained-glass windows designed by Kempe, both installed in 1889. This most prolific designer is only

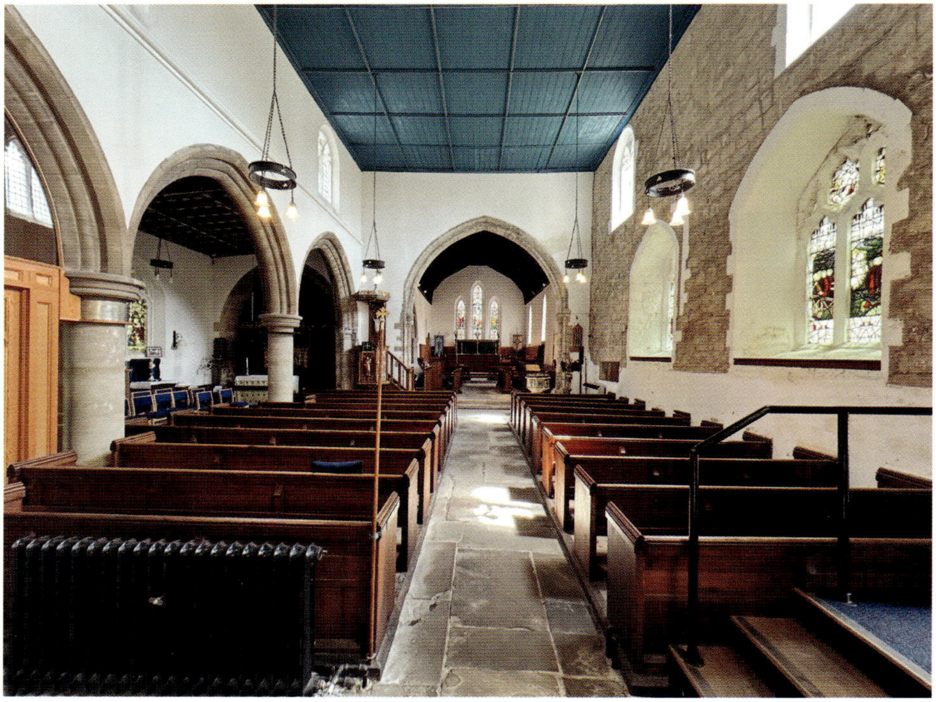

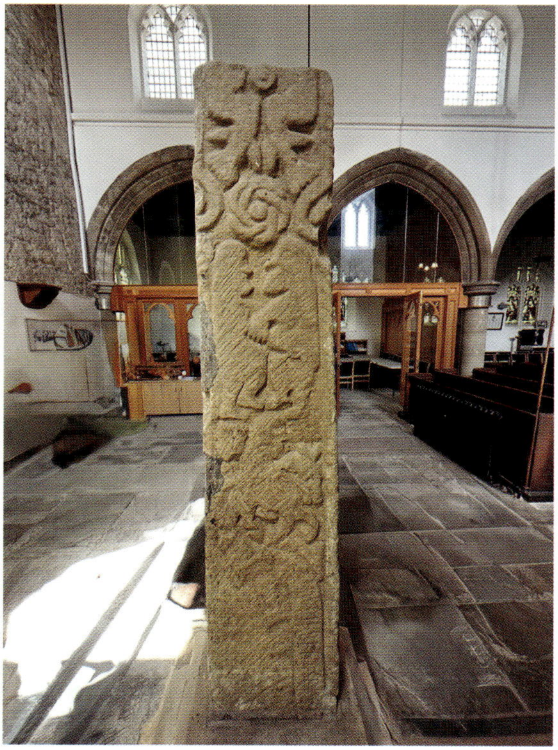

Above: Crowle. Interior looking east. The Georgian flat ceiling is quite unexpected. The south wall is the oldest part of the church, dating from the Norman period.

Left: Crowle. The extraordinary pre-Conquest grave marker with a mixture of Saxon and Viking iconography. This face shows two figures embracing.

represented in thirty Lincolnshire churches, so is not as well known here as he is in other counties. The blue ceiling of the nave hides an eighteenth-century roof and at one time the church must have been of the 'high church' persuasion as the early twentieth-century furnishings show. The altar rails, panelling and altar are especially appealing and an inscription records that they date from 1935. The single memorial of interest is the brass plate which remembers the Stovin family. However, it is the standing stone by the door that we have really come to see. Its survival is due to it being reused as rubble when the Normans built the church. Now freestanding, we can see how impressive it must have looked when first erected, possibly in the late ninth or early tenth century. The carvings on it are difficult to interpret, but we can see two figures facing each other with a third person on a horse beneath. There is a damaged text said to be a Saxon form of runic inscription incorporating the words for 'corpse monument', making this a graveyard marker. Sadly, when the Normans reused the stone they chiselled some of the carving off. The reverse side is carved with a deep interlace design.

16. Deeping St James, Priory Church of St James

The Fens are well known for their monastic history, but I suspect that Deeping is less well known than Crowland, Thorney and Peterborough. Yet here are the remains of a substantial twelfth-century building, the church founded as a

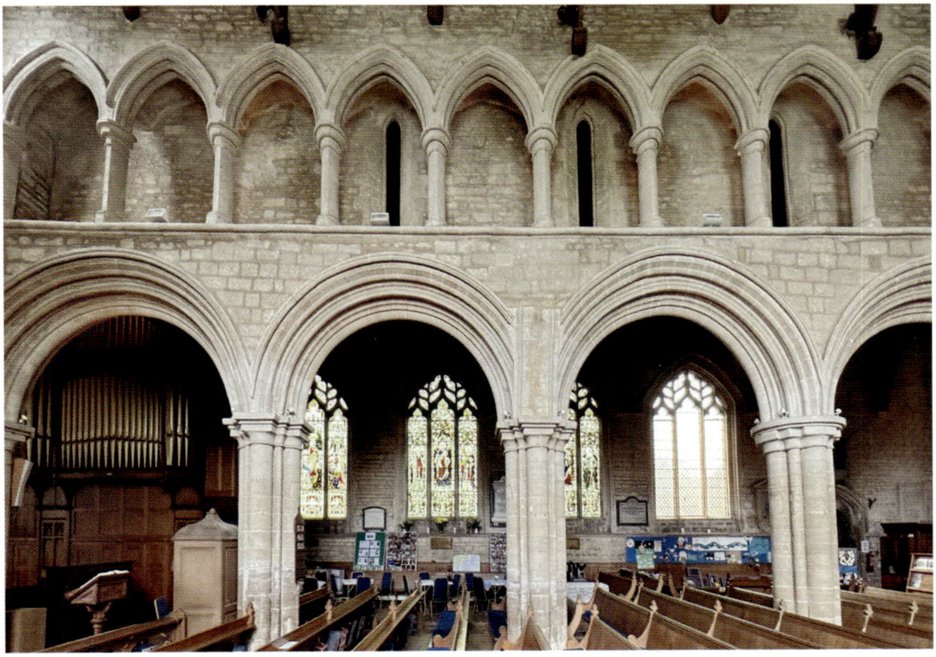

Deeping St James. A former monastery where we see the south wall of the nave. Sturdy Norman arcades are topped by a wall passage in the then new Gothic form with pointed arches, making the whole construction late twelfth or very early thirteenth century. The windows in the wall passage were originally external, but the south aisle roof was later raised in height.

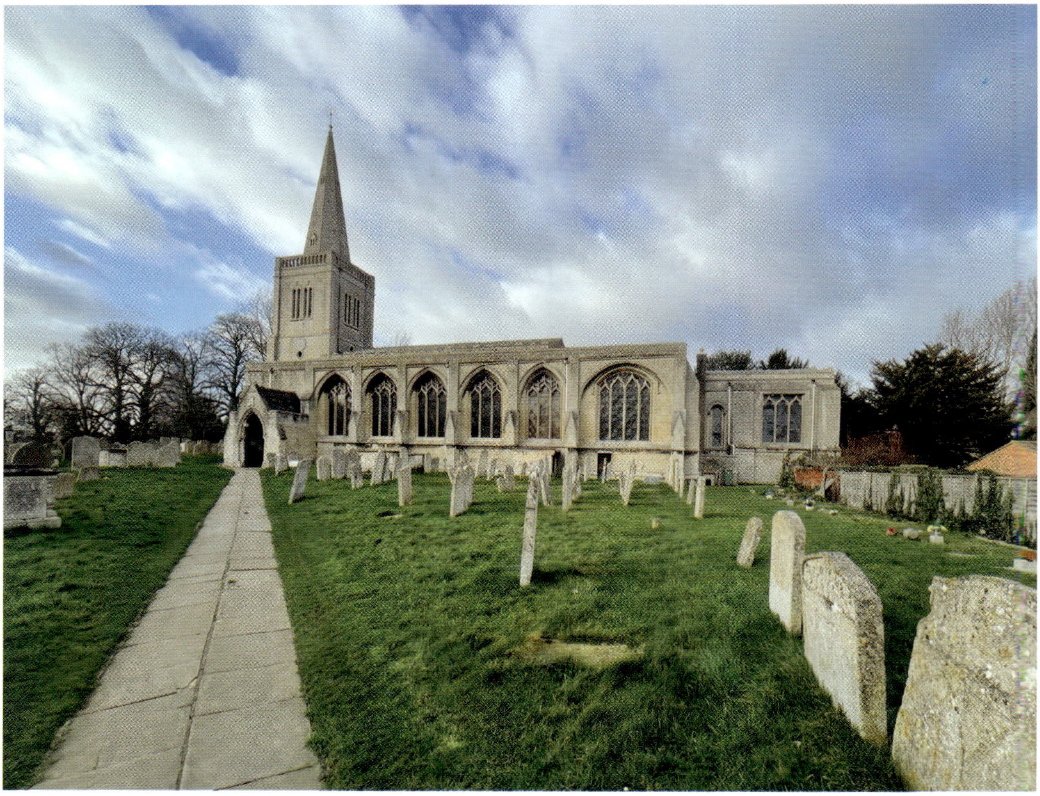

Deeping St James. Viewed from the south. Since its monastic days the church has been considerably reduced in size, but the huge fourteenth-century windows are testament to its former glories.

monastery by Baldwin FitzGilbert in 1139. He is depicted in stained glass over the pulpit by Thomas Curtis of the firm of Ward and Hughes. If the tower looks a little out of place it is because it is a Georgian rebuild, made using the same Barnack stone that the whole building is constructed with. The huge Norman tub font with interlaced arcaded sides, though much recut, shows that this was not just a Benedictine monastery but a parish church as well. The finest Norman architecture are the windows in the south wall of the chancel with their bold rere-arches and the smaller arches beneath which originally formed a series of sedilia, or seats. Incorporated into the design is a double piscina for the priest to wash his fingers and chalice, which dates from the thirteenth century. At about the same time the south aisle was enlarged and the arches dividing them, now leaning wildly as a result of subsidence, were rebuilt with a triforium stage of pointed openings above. The chancel contains two effigies of benefactors to the priory, both of which are well worn and must have been kept outside at some stage. Sadly, their names were not recorded. In the nave is a hudd, a graveyard shelter for an eighteenth-century parson which allowed him to conduct funerals at the graveside without getting his wig wet. It is a rare survivor; others may be found in Norfolk,

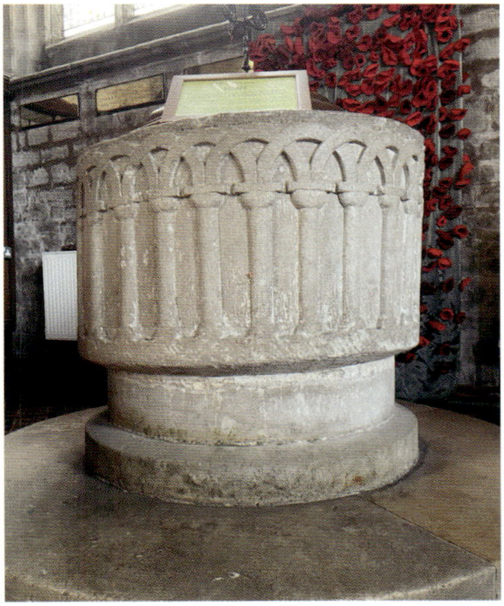

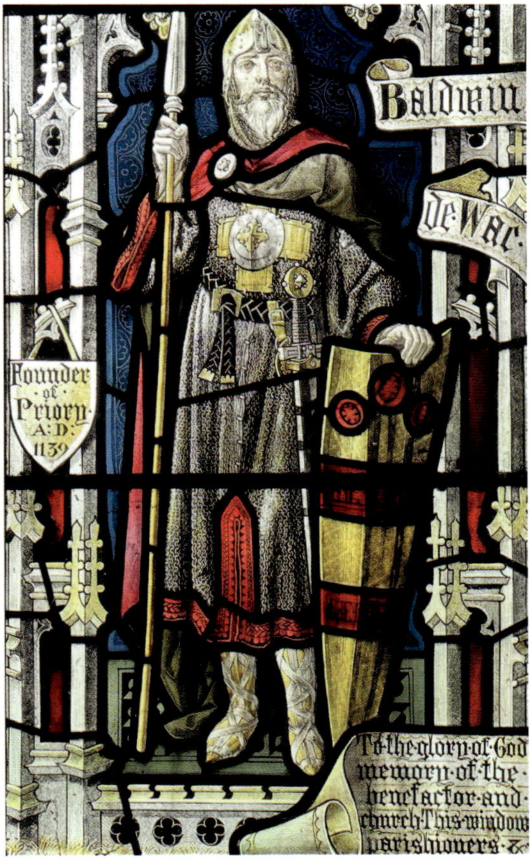

Above: Deeping St James.
The twelfth-century font with interlaced decoration reminds us that this was a parochial church as well as a monastery.

Right: Deeping St James. The monastery was founded in 1139 by Baldwin, depicted in this Victorian stained-glass window by the firm of Ward and Hughes.

Yorkshire and Kent. The medieval patrons of the church were Thorney Abbey and, after the Reformation, the Dukes of Norfolk, so they are not represented by monuments. The most prominent local family then was the Coopers, who have their vault at the west end and who are commemorated by multiple inscriptions on the west wall.

17. Denton, St Andrew

An estate church of the Welby family. The building has more Perpendicular work of the fifteenth century than most churches in this part of the county, the most obvious example of this being the castellated capitals on the arcade which add so much character to the interior. However, there is still fourteenth century work to find including the sedilia and piscina in the chancel. There too is a low-relief fourteenth-century effigy of a priest. Just inside the door is a delightful memorial to John Blyth (d. 1602), the effigy rather squashed in under the backplate. On the front of the freestone chest are pictures of his wife and their six children, each of whom is named. The Corinthian pillars carrying the entablature show that the classical style had now taken over as the must-have design. Opposite it the monument to Richard Welby (d. 1713) is of marble and shows how tastes had changed in a hundred years. The Blyth figure held a prayerbook, but now there is no suggestion that Welby is at prayer. Instead, he is standing proudly whilst two angels offer a coronet of everlasting life. Its carver was Thomas Green of Camberwell, whose monuments are frequently on a majestic scale. When Mary, John's wife, died (she was a great heiress according to the inscription) a local stone carver was brought in to add her details on a blank panel. It is an amateur job compared to the original, with poor layout and a reversed 'N'. There is much Victorian stained glass in the church, several windows being by the firm of Ward and Hughes, but the best is that by Kempe in the chancel, where his signature of a wheatsheaf can be found on the edge a third of the way up the left-hand side. The extraordinary carved wooden reredos, which shows grapevines, was carved by the Arts and Crafts artist Lady Nina Cust, who had grown up in the village, and forms a memorial to her mother. A member of the famous 'Souls' group of

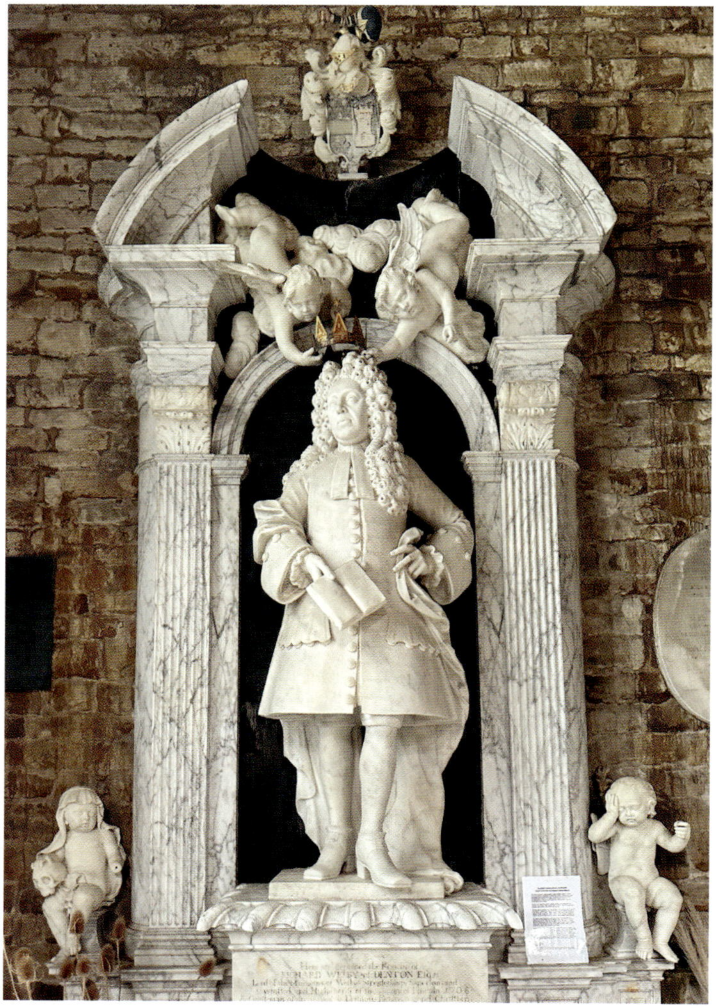

Denton. Monument in marble to Richard Welby, who died in 1713. Angels descending from the clouds offer him a crown of glory whilst two disconsolate cherubs sit below.

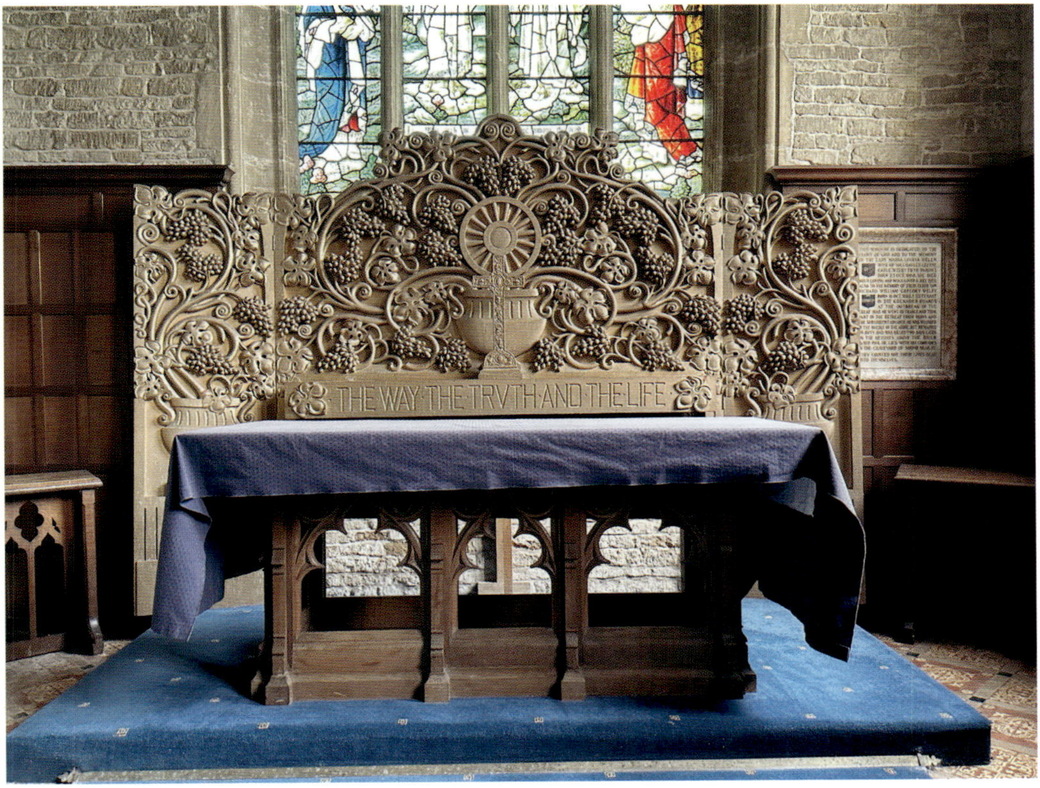

Denton. The enormous Arts and Crafts reredos carved by Lady Nina Cust (1867–1955) depicts the vine and grapes of Holy Communion.

aesthetes, her story was told by Jane Dismore in the book *Tangled Souls*. Beneath the tower are seven funeral hatchments, each carried at the funeral of a member of the Welby family. It is a good set to study as it shows the difference between a married man (black left-hand side) and a married woman (black right-hand side).

18. Donington, St Mary and the Holy Rood

In the summer of 2024, there was much excitement here when the remains of Matthew Flinders, navigator and cartographer, were buried in the village of his birth over 200 years after his death. He had originally been buried in London, but when his grave was excavated in advance of the construction of HS2 the opportunity was taken to 'bring him home'. He had always been remembered in the church with a simple naval memorial in the chancel, but now his grave in the north aisle attracts many visitors. It depicts his ship circumnavigating Australia and his much-travelled cat, Trim, who also appears on his statue in Donington Market Place. A window designed by John Hayward in 1979 also recalls his travels and companions, whilst a window in the south aisle, also by Hayward, is more typical of his style and shows St Hugh of Lincoln, Our Lady

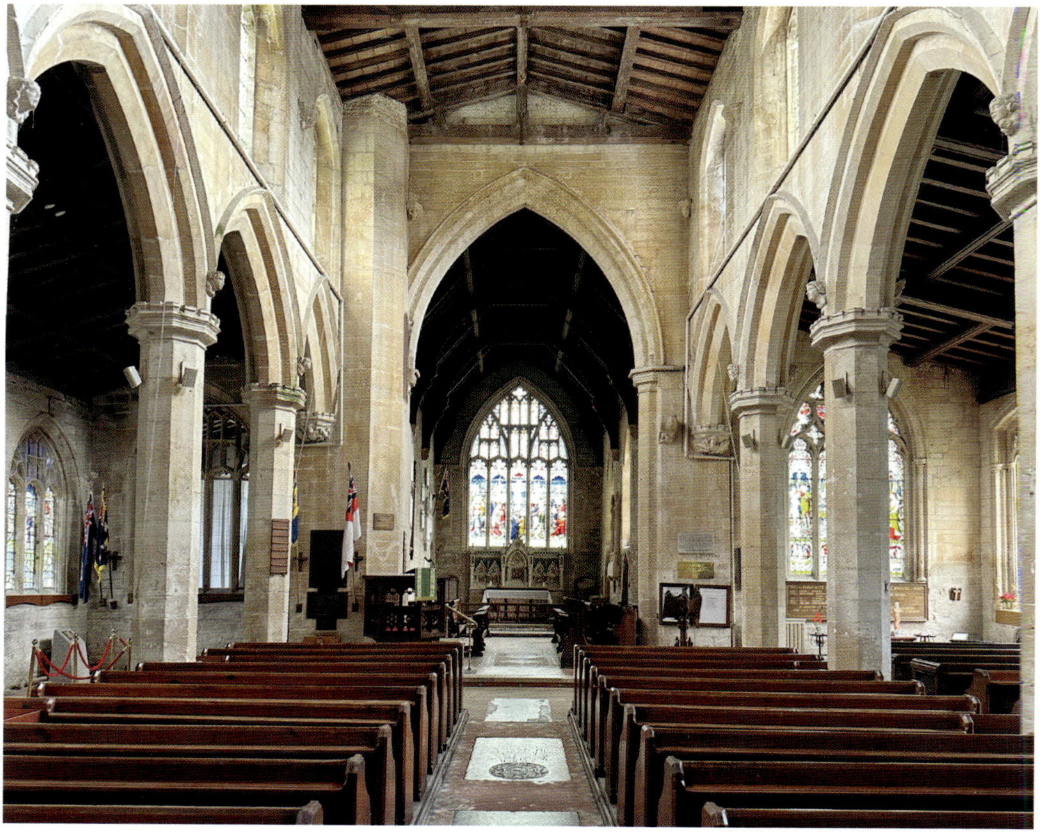

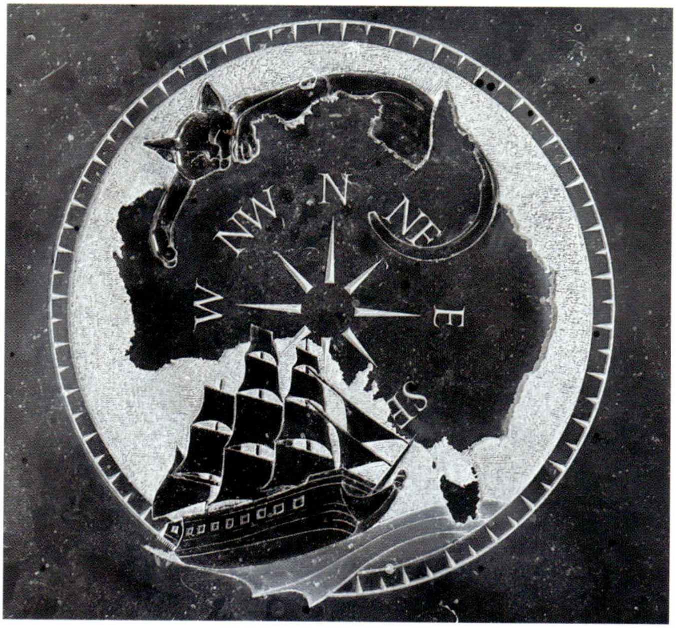

Above: Donington. The corbel to the right of the chancel arch shows where the rood beam would have crossed the arch. It is at the same level as the door to the rood loft just visible on the left. This in turn was reached by its own staircase which continued up to give access to the roof.

Left: The modern ledger stone to Captain Matthew Flinders (1774–1814), who was reinterred here in 2024. It depicts his cat, Trim, embracing Australia, which Flinders circumnavigated in the eighteenth century.

and Child and St Swithun. Aside from the Flinders connection, the church has much to offer. The arcades have castellated capitals (see entry 17), which raises the architectural importance, together with the fact that the internal walls of the church are constructed in ashlar or smooth blocks of stone rather than the more usual rubble. The dominant feature of the interior is the thick rood loft staircase to the north of the chancel arch, which is carried up to access the roof flats. Lead roofs lend themselves to graffiti and in the porch are displayed sections removed from older roof structures which show initials, dates and the outlines of feet. It was very common for people to trace around their shoes or hands as evidence of having been up there, and this small display shows the various ways in which people achieved this using knives and nails. At the rear of the church is a Hudd or graveside shelter to keep an eighteenth-century clergyman dry during a burial (see also entries 16 and 37). Two oddities are to be found in the church. Firstly, a stone bench arm in the chancel, which dates from the thirteenth century, must have come from an early sedilia, and secondly a table carved of Tasmanian pine, which originally belonged to Tasmania House in London. The churches of Lincolnshire often surprise us.

19. Edenham, St Michael

This rather unassuming church set on a busy road hides its fame. For this is the estate church for Grimsthorpe Castle, the stately home of the Willoughby d'Eresby family and as such contains an astonishing collection of monuments. You step down into a vast church of the thirteenth century with light flooding in through the clerestory windows onto an impressive angel roof. Over the chancel arch is a huge late Hanoverian royal arms, in the position that most churches chose after the Restoration of the Monarchy. As you enter the church, opposite is a Romanesque doorway, which is something of an interloper, having been brought here in 1967 from a farm nearby. Next to it is the oldest object to be found at Edenham, a fragment of a Saxon churchyard cross. Hidden high on the walls in the south aisle are two more Saxon carved fragments, proving that there has been an important church here for over a thousand years. Displayed under the tower are five medieval effigies, now much weathered, dating from the 1300s, showing the deceased with straight legs in an attitude of prayer. Nearby, set into the wall, is a small carved panel showing three water carriers, or bouchets. These form part of the shields of arms of many medieval families, but here they probably relate to the de Ros family and must have formed part of a large late medieval monument. Overhead hang two helms, medieval helmets made to be carried in the funeral processions of armigerous men. The east end of the north aisle is partitioned off as the private pew of the big house. It contains the monument to Robert Bertie (d. 1642), displaying his emblem of the Order of the Garter as well as cannon and other military symbols from the Wars of the Three Kingdoms. Later family members are commemorated in even more elaborate form. The 1st Duke of Ancaster (d. 1723) stands in Roman toga, his monument signed by two famous names in English sculpture – Henry Scheemakers and Henry Cheere. The latter also carved the monument of the 2nd Duke (d. 1741), who appeared in a

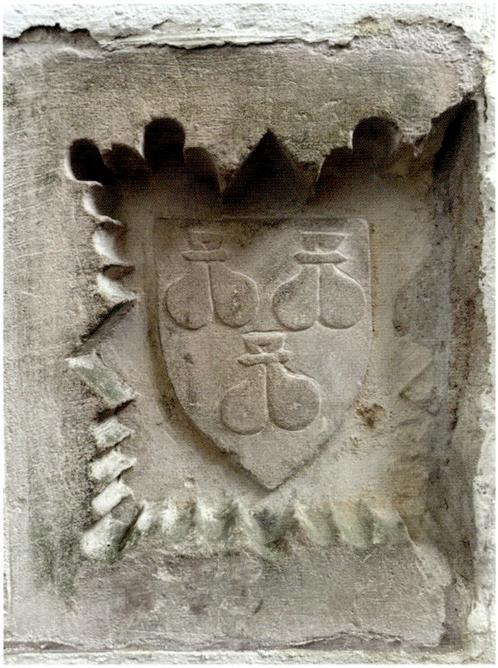

Left: Edenham. These strange-looking objects are water buckets, or bouchets, which form part of the heraldry of the de Ros family and would originally have formed part of a monument.

Below: Edenham. Interior looking east. The arcades are a grand thirteenth-century design with clustered shafts whilst the angel roof is fifteenth century. Over the chancel arch is a fine Georgian royal shield of arms.

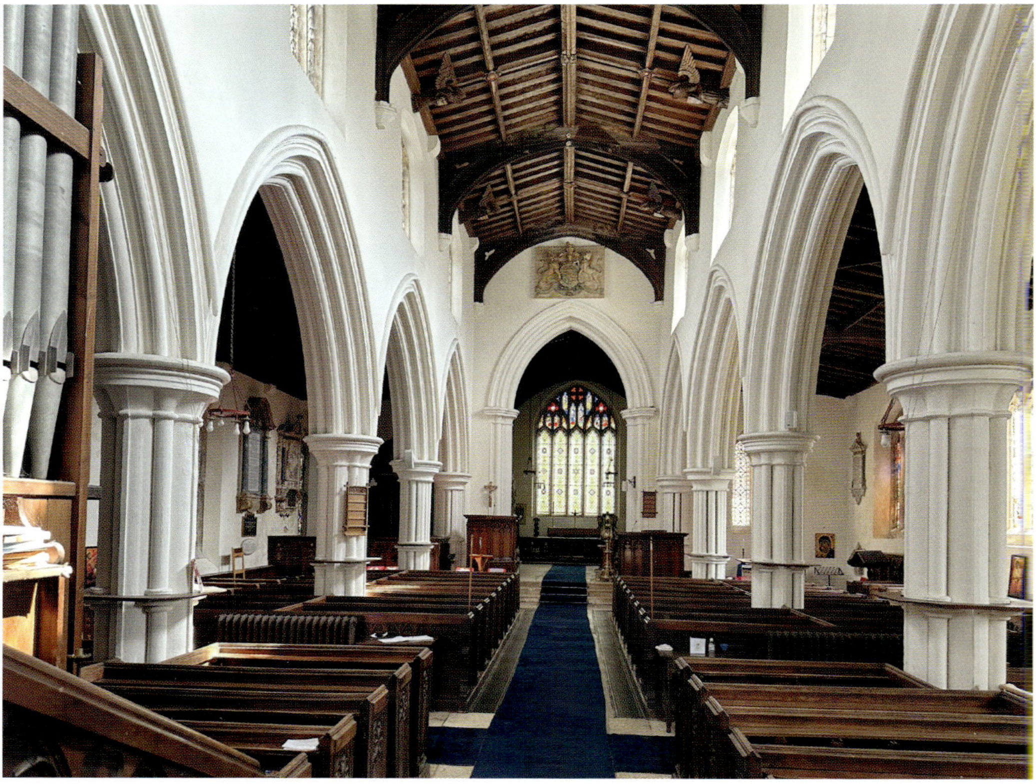

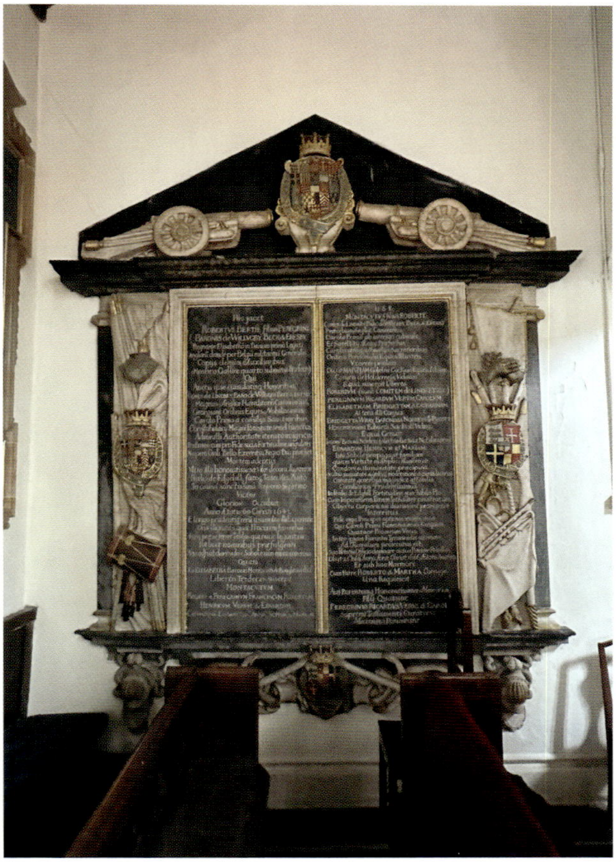

Edenham. The monument to Robert Bertie, 1st Earl of Lindsey, who was killed at the Battle of Edgehill (1642) during the Wars of the Three Kingdoms. His son, who was captured by the Parliamentarians whilst tending to his dying father, is also commemorated, their tablet framed by military trophies.

portrait medallion. The most impressive monument, however, is to Lord Robert Willoughby (d. 1738), which takes the form of a large black sarcophagus set on lions' paws, above which are seven portrait busts. The lengthy inscription tells the life stories of his children.

20. Gautby, All Saints

This part of the county feels very remote, yet Gautby was once a great estate with the big house, home to the Vyner family, in the flat land to the south of the church. Sadly, only features of its landscaped grounds and stables survive, the house having been demolished in 1872. It would have looked out onto this diminutive red-brick church, rebuilt in 1754 – probably on Norman greenstone foundations. The lovely yellow painted interior is well cared for and sets off the glorious Georgian plasterwork very well. There are plain benches and one box pew, and a two-decker pulpit reputedly brought from Skelton in North Yorkshire, which was another estate owned by the same family. In the early twentieth century the churchmanship here took a swerve upwards so there are statues and religious pictures dotted about, and a prominent rood group hanging from

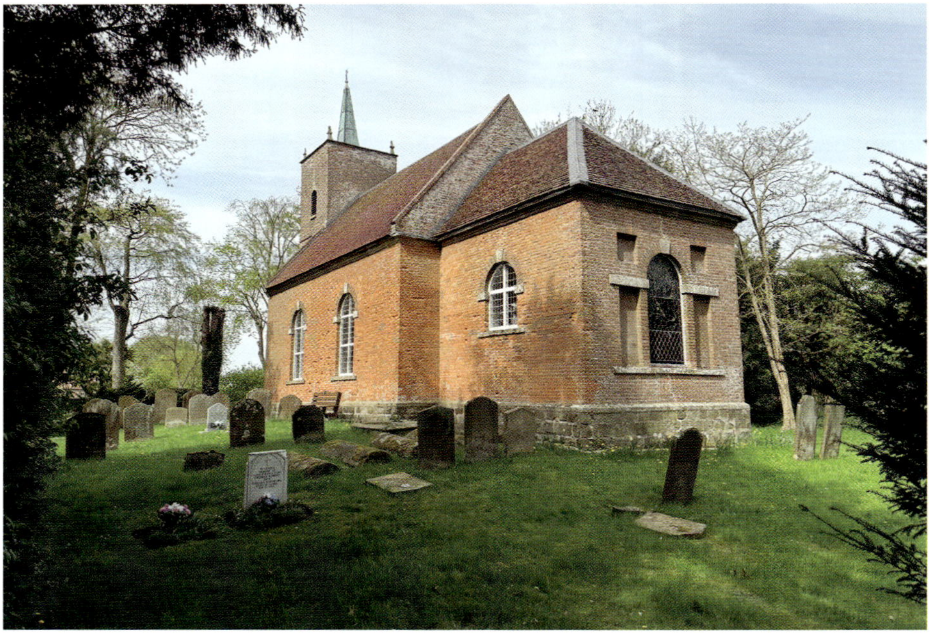

Gautby. Built in 1754, it is one of many brick Lincolnshire churches of that date. The chancel is larger than one would have expected, but by looking at the base of the walls you can see that it was built on earlier Norman foundations.

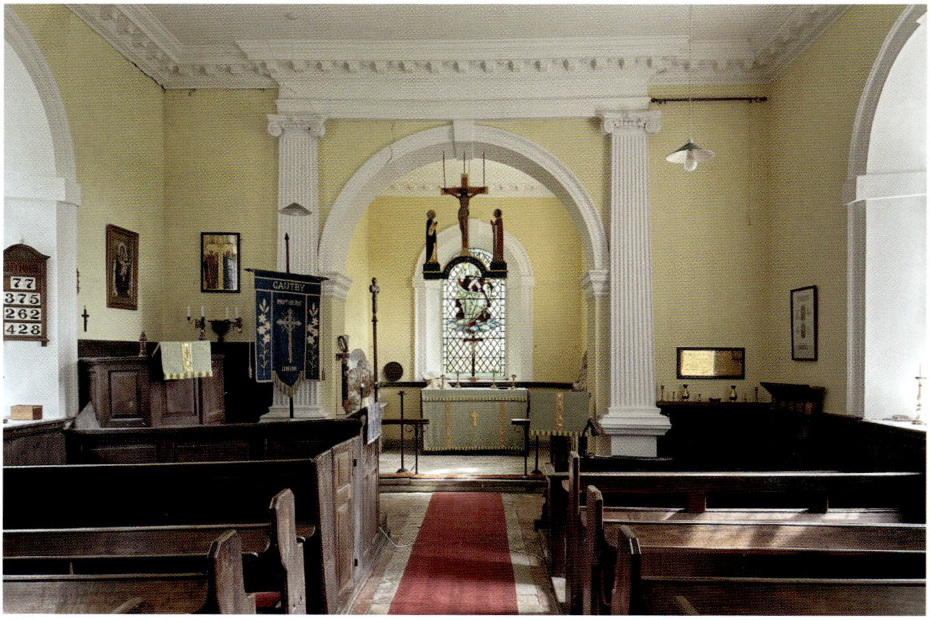

Gautby. The homely interior is dominated by the plaster chancel arch. The open benches were for the tenants, whilst the box pew by the pulpit would have been accommodation for the lords of the manor – the Vyner family.

the chancel arch. The east window is also twentieth century, by William Morris of Westminster, signed in the bottom corner, depicting the risen Christ as King of Heaven. Either side of the window are two unexpected interlopers. These effigies of members of the Vyner family were originally in the Church of St Mary Woolnoth in the City of London. They represent two Thomas Vyners. The elder is on the south side, proudly displaying the chain which represents his position as Lord Mayor of London. He was a goldsmith and Keeper of the Royal Mint. The other effigy commemorates his son. It is suggested that these are the work of Jasper Latham, the master mason who worked on the rebuilding of St Paul's Cathedral. He certainly worked for the Vyner family in the city, so it would seem possible that these monuments might be by him. It is not recorded when they were moved here. The floor of the chancel is covered with memorials to those members of the family buried in the vault beneath. These include the famous Frederick Vyner, killed, together with other English gentlemen, by Greek brigands in 1870 after being held hostage and who died in a botched rescue attempt. The church on the Vyner's Yorkshire state was rebuilt in his memory. Thank goodness the same didn't happen here.

21. Gedney, St Mary Magdalene

Throughout our exploration of churches, one of the most important things we need to remember is who the patrons were who financed the buildings we are seeing. Sometimes it was a wealthy wool merchant, or a town guild, or a monastery. In Gedney's case it was Croyland Abbey, a wealthy foundation that used its influence to rebuild the churches in its care. This is why such an enormous church stands on the edge of the Fens. The earliest part of the church is the massive west tower, which was originally designed to have a spire. Why this was never constructed is a mystery, but possibly it was felt that the extra weight would have been unsustainable on this soft ground. The church is entered through its original fourteenth-century door. This is one of the treasures of Lincolnshire, carrying an inscription in Latin above the tiny wicket door: 'The Peace of Christ be on this House and all dwelling in it. Here is our rest.' It is worth looking at the back of the door as well; here you'll find the original bronze lock, which also carries an inscription, this time from the locksmith John Pete, who it seems made his lock unpickable! The church is barn like with a high multi-bossed ceiling that shows the honest repairs of centuries. Above the tower arch you can see the scar of the original fourteenth-century roof before it was replaced by the clerestory and present structure in the fifteenth century. Whilst the base of the font is dated 1664, this must refer to a different structure. The puritans didn't agree with infant baptism so threw many fonts out during the 1650s, which is why many had to be replaced after the Restoration of the Monarchy. In the south aisle is a charming brass to a woman of about 1400 with an adoring dog at her feet. Sadly, the inscription and heraldry is missing, so we are unable to identify her. The most impressive monument is the alabaster tablet to the Elizabethans Adlard and Cassandra Welby, which shows them kneeling at two prayer desks. The inscription tells us that it was erected in 1605, in the third year of the reign

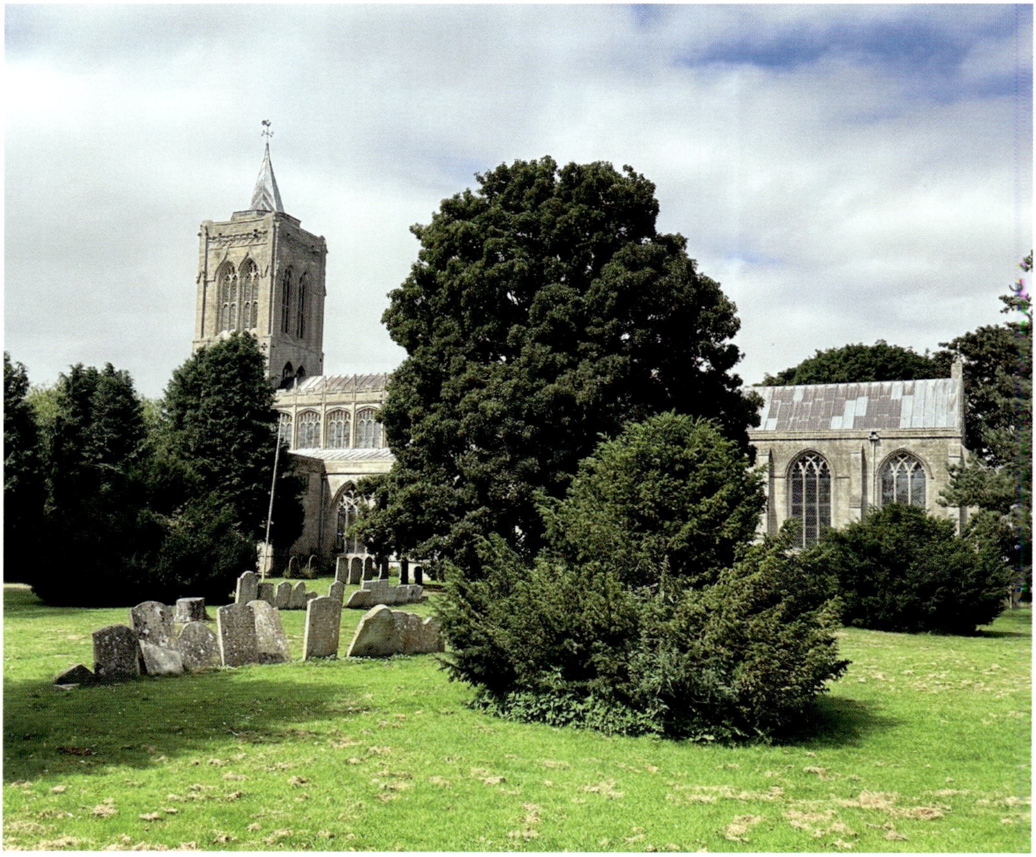

Gedney. A cathedral-like church of massive proportions in the far south-east of the county, taking its cue from the wealth of the Wash before even greater glories came with wool production.

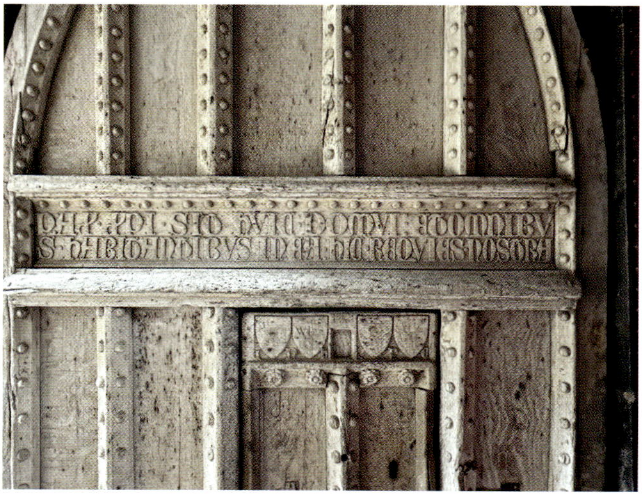

Gedney. The fourteenth-century south door has an inscription carved into its outer face asking for peace on all who enter it. The shields below would have been painted with the heraldry of the donors. The whole door is brightly painted.

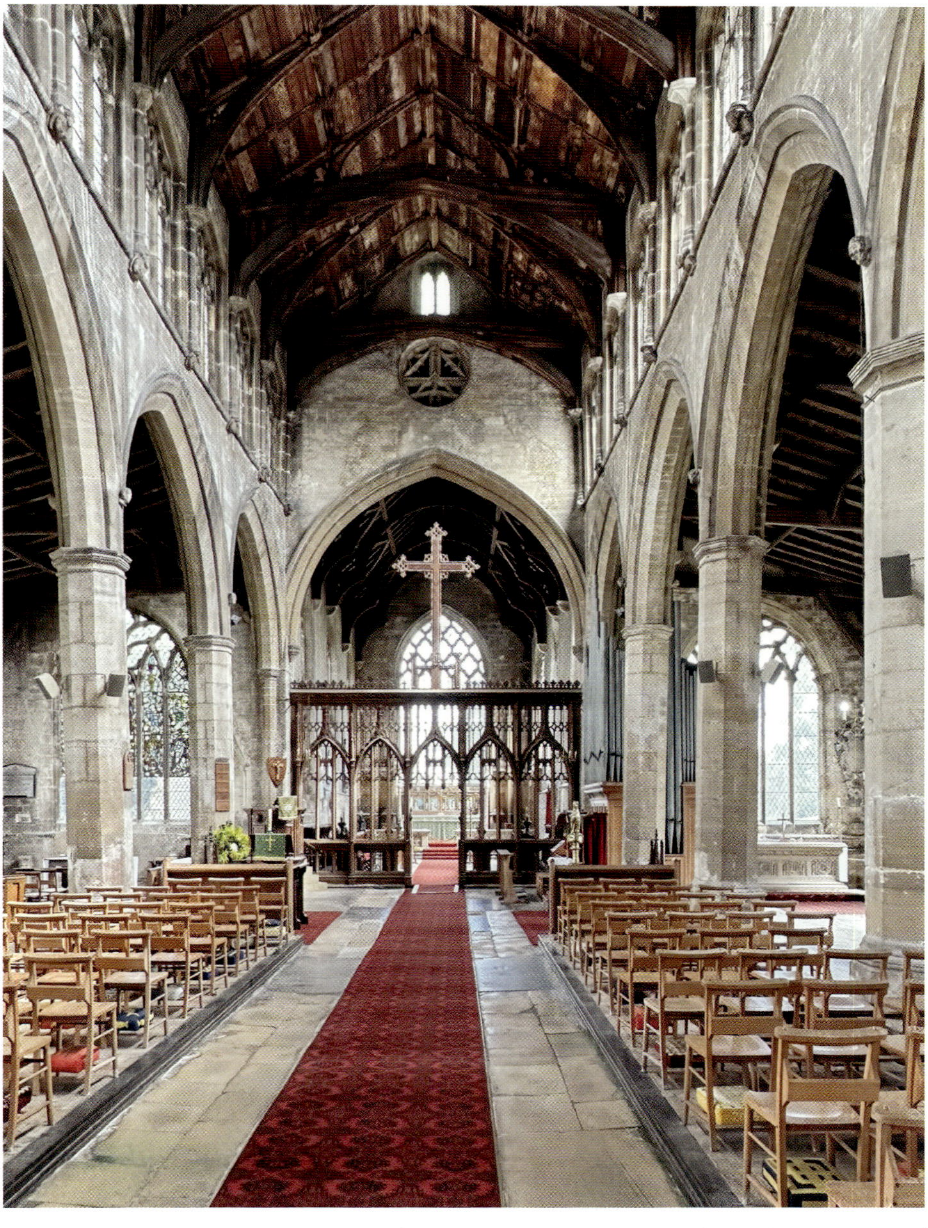

Gedney. The nave and chancel are both fourteenth century in date, the former having a row of clerestory windows from the start. The rood screen, with its plain cross, is Victorian.

of James I, who had already reigned as King James VI of Scotland for thirty-eight years. No doubt Adlard's son, who commissioned the monument, was showing his allegiance to the Stuart king. The east window of the north aisle contains a large number of medieval glass fragments that once made up a tree of Jesse. How impressive the church must have looked when all its windows were full of colour.

22. Grantham, St Wulfram

This is one of the best churches to see the development of the Decorated style of architecture from 1250 to 1350, as the previous church was completely rebuilt during this period. Blocked windows from a Norman clerestory can be seen over the later arcades halfway down the nave. Those aside, what we see is the result of several building campaigns, not designed as a set piece but as the result of changes in plans and designs by successive generations. The windows demonstrate this admirably. On the west front, either side of the main door, are two windows in

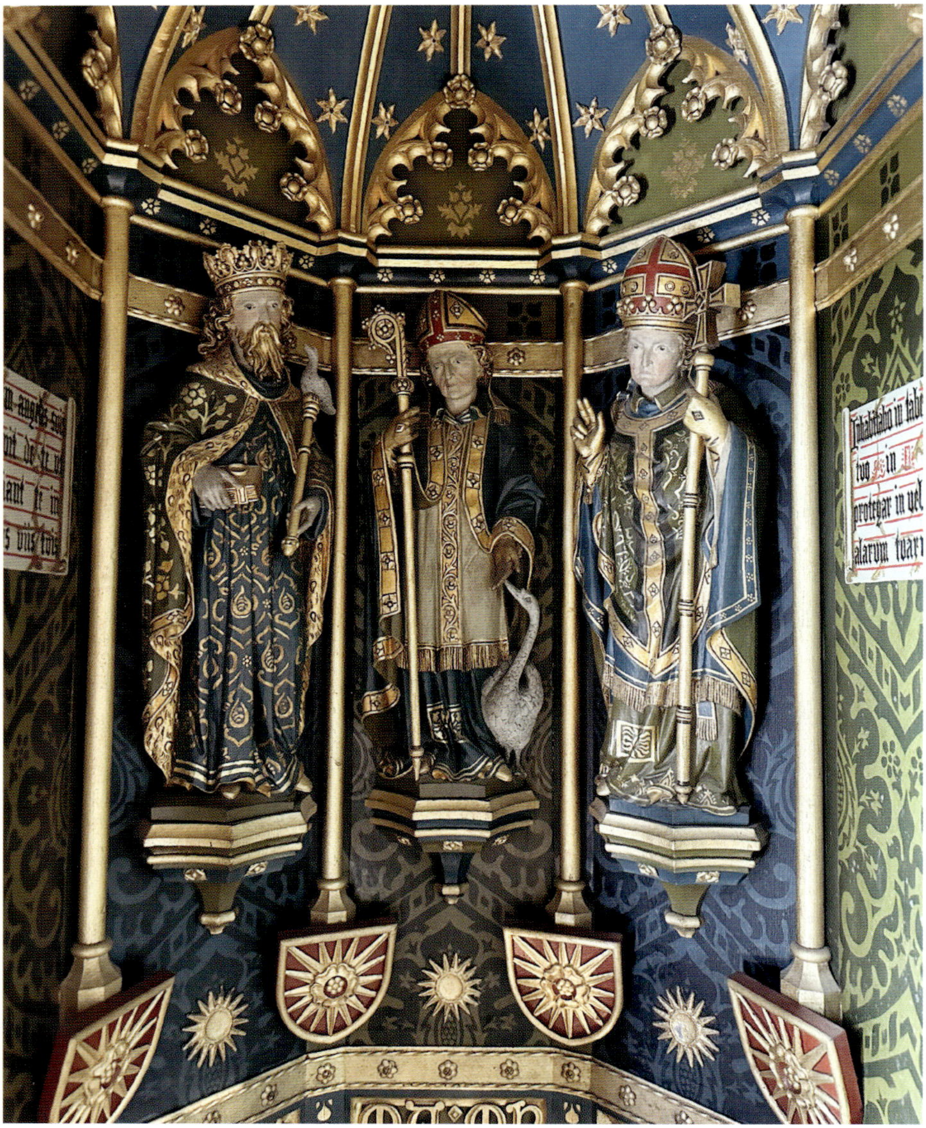

Grantham. This scene is within the font cover of 1899 designed by Sir Walter Tapper. It depicts St Edward the Confessor, St Hugh of Lincoln and St Wulfram, whose shrine stands in this church.

the geometric style with a central window of intersecting tracery. As we progress down the church the windows change to flowing tracery of different designs. Only the Perpendicular windows at the east end are of a later period. The windows are mainly filled with nineteenth- and twentieth-century glass, some of it of excellent quality. Two aisle windows opposite each other are by John Hayward, one of the last century's best-loved artists, and represent Peace and the Seven Sacraments. The first thing the visitor sees is the huge font cover made in 1899 by Sir Walter Tapper. If you're lucky, it will be open to show the richly painted interior with images of St Edward the Confessor, St Hugh of Lincoln and St Wulfram, whose shrine stands in this church. The roofs of the church are all nineteenth century and were designed by Sir Gilbert Scott, as was the rood screen. Above the kitchen area are two royal arms – a rare one for Queen Elizabeth I, the other of King Charles II. The south-east corner of the church forms the Lady Chapel, where the altar frontal is of especial interest. It was designed by Sir Walter Tapper and made by Watts and Co. of London in 1924. The symbolism relates to Our Lady, including her representation as the 'Morning Star'. In the same chapel stands the modern shrine of the Frenchman St Wulfram. After his death and burial in France in AD 703 his

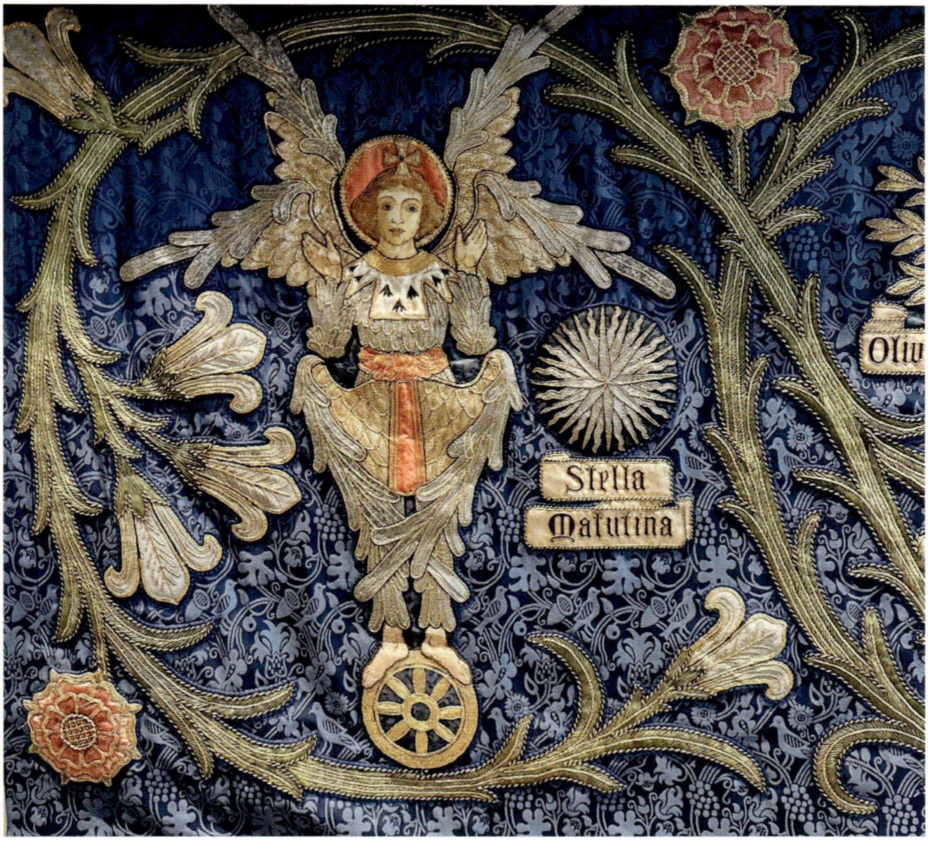

The altar frontal in the Lady Chapel dates from 1924 and was made by Watts and Co. It depicts Our Lady as the 'Morning Star' and was designed by Sir Walter Tapper.

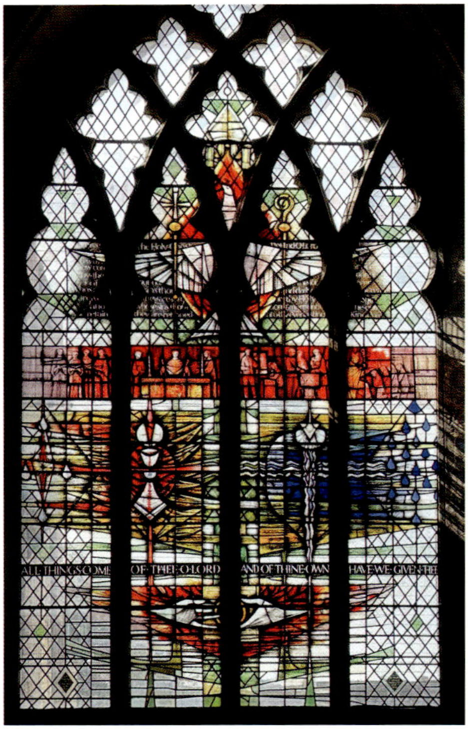

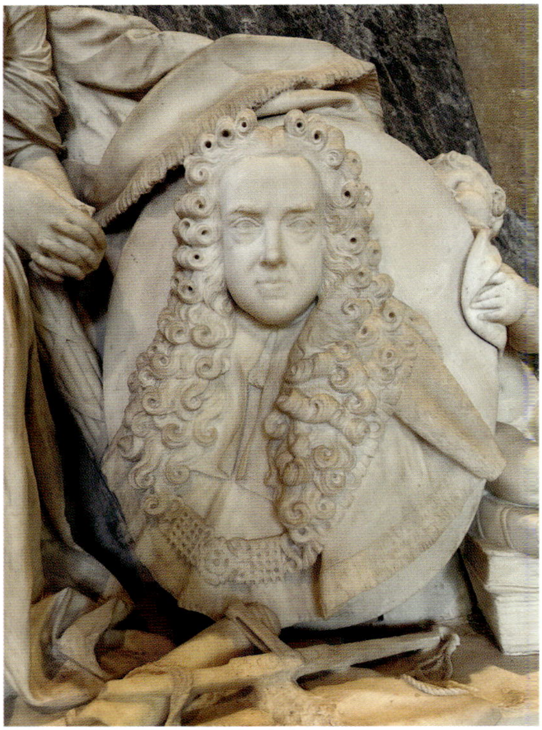

Above left: Grantham. John Hayward (1929–2007) was the designer of two windows in the church. This one (1974) depicts the Seven Sacraments of Baptism, Ordination, Marriage, Holy Communion, Confirmation, the Last Rights and Confession.

Above right: Grantham. Monument to Sir Dudly Ryder (d. 1756), a portrait medallion by Henry Cheere.

tomb became a place of pilgrimage and in the late Norman period his arm was taken to Croyland Abbey in Lincolnshire, but following a fire there it was brought to Grantham where it was displayed until the Reformation. The church contains some impressive monuments including one to the judge Sir Dudley Ryder (d. 1756), designed by Sir Henry Cheere (see entry 19). Ryder sadly died before a promised peerage could be bestowed upon him. Cheere also designed the monument bristling with military symbolism to William Cust, who was killed in 1747 when he was struck by a cannonball aboard HMS *Elizabeth* during the War of Jenkins' Ear.

23. Hainton, St Mary

The church stands in a manicured churchyard not far from the hall, which has been in the hands of the Heneage family for 600 years. Whilst they were a recusant family for much of that time, the parish church remained the place in which their rites of passage were conducted. It is their monuments that we have come to see, the majority of them housed in the north chapel which is separated from the rest of the church by seventeenth-century iron railings. The church itself is mainly a rebuild of 1847 by E. J. Willson, who is buried in the churchyard and who designed several nearby estate buildings. It is a lovely structure but lacks the patina of age which we expect to find in a country church. The earliest monument is to John Heneage (d. 1530) and may be found on the north wall of the chancel. He was firstly a servant of Thomas Wolsey but afterwards became a Gentleman of the Bedchamber to Henry VIII. It takes the form of an Easter sepulchre, which suggests it may have been moved slightly west of its original location as it is no longer adjacent to the altar. On the wall above the tomb chest is a brass representation of the deceased, depicted wearing a tabard and with his wife and daughter. The prominent shield of arms in the centre is a replacement for a representation of the Holy Trinity and, in fact, everything apart from the inscription plate is a clever replacement. It is interesting to consider John's rather dubious role in the royal household, which was as Groom of the Stool – he attended the king on his toilet. From here the family trail leads into the chapel, where there are several monuments of note. Most prominent is the freestanding alabaster effigy of George Heneage (d. 1595) whose brightly painted heraldry must be part of a later repainting. The carved detail is amazing – just look at his huge lower eyelids. The alabaster came from the quarry at Fauld near Burton upon Trent and was

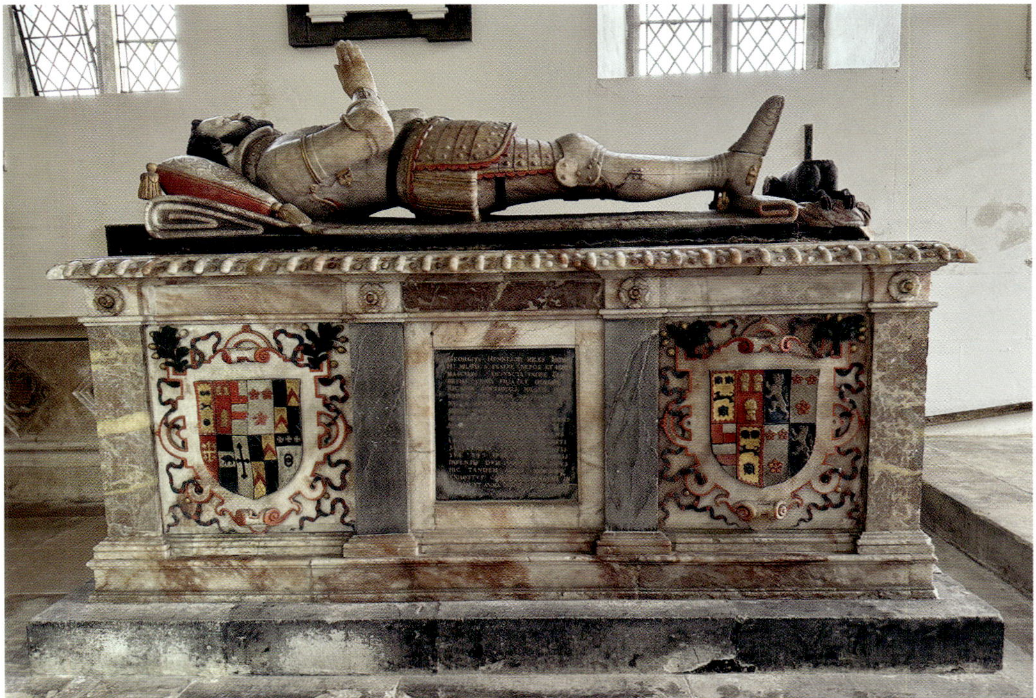

Hainton. The monument to Sir George Heneage (d. 1595) carved in alabaster from the Fauld Quarry in Staffordshire which was then painted to cover its imperfections. Heneage was a former ambassador to France.

possibly carved by Garrett Hollemans who, with his son Jasper, had a studio there. It is a pity that it has been damaged in recent times. The largest monument in the chapel is to George Heneage (d. 1731) and comprises a portrait bust together with one of each of his two wives, Mary and Elizabeth. It is signed 'CB' and it has been suggested that this may have been an Italian sculptor. The fulsome inscription tells us of his qualities and hasn't allowed much space for information about his wives, who are commemorated on separate marble tablets; from these we learn that they were both heiresses. His son George married an Italian, which may explain why the commission for this memorial went there. There are about a dozen Heneage monuments of note.

24. Haltham-on-Bain, St Benedict

This small, unpretentious church provides enough architectural clues to keep the avid church crawler busy for hours. It must have had two periods in its history when money was available: about 1300 and again in 1820. Apart from that, it has tottered along with minor repairs and adornments. In the south porch is the oldest feature here, a Romanesque tympanum carved with a variety of subjects in a crude

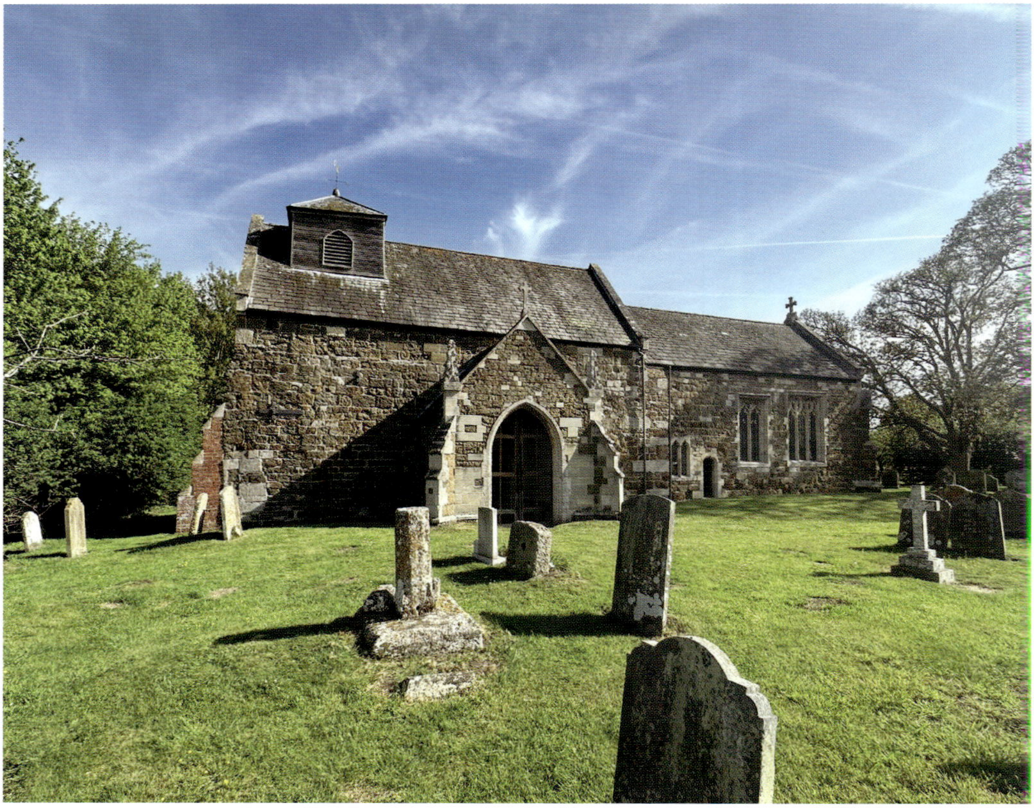

Haltham-on-Bain. Now cared for by the Churches Conservation Trust, this church is built of the local soft 'greenstone', a sandstone that develops a green tinge due to the presence of glauconite.

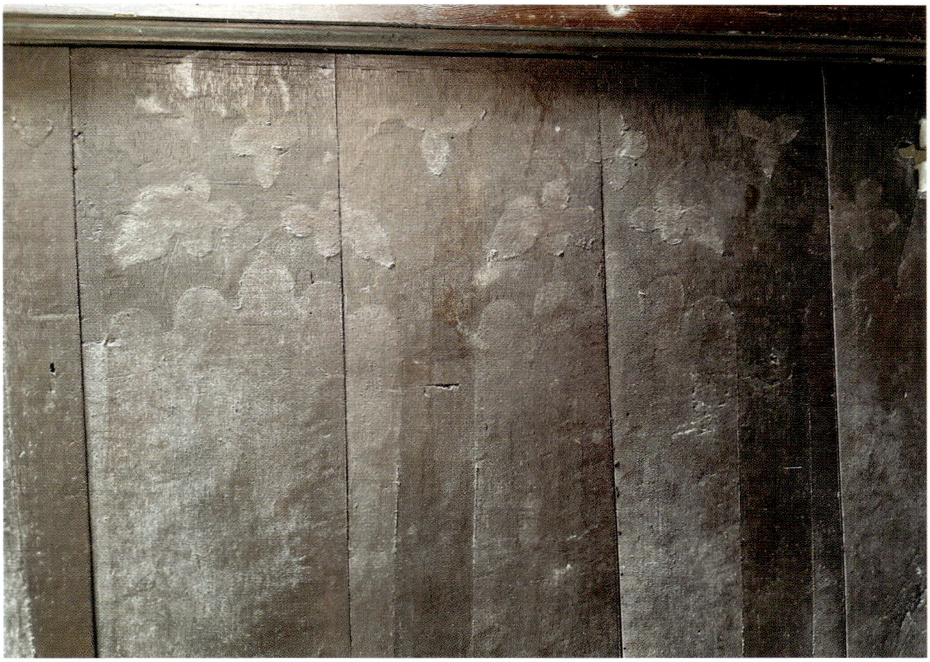

Haltham-on-Bain. Some of the boards from the former rood screen now reset nearby show the outline of medieval tracery as a ghost under nineteenth-century varnish.

style, the best of which is a decorative knot. The church has little stained glass, so is wonderfully light, but the dark wood fittings sombre the mood somewhat. The east window is the showpiece of the stonemason's art in about 1300, having four lights with quatrefoils and mouchettes above, and was probably the gift of a single benefactor. Around the same time, or slightly earlier, is the arcade to the north aisle with deeply carved acanthus leaves, one of which incorporates the fleur-de-lys emblem. The base of the bell turret is enclosed with timber planks, and on the east facing enclosure is the ghostly outline of the royal arms of King Charles II with the date '1663' and fragments of the Decalogue. These panels must have once fitted into the top of the chancel arch following the removal of the rood screen. The latter survives in dismembered parts across the east end of the nave. The top tracery is still in situ but brought down to a lower level, whilst the dado and crenelations are now built into pews in the nave and north aisle. You can pick out two tiny squints that would have allowed a kneeling worshipper to look through the base of the screen to the elevation of the host, although the planks into which they are carved are now placed at 90 degrees. If you have a torch, you'll find that these planks were once covered in paintwork; petals of flowers survive and some outline tracery panels where the applied design has long been removed, leaving a bare outline with remains of glue. Throughout the church are little carved stone heads, none of which seem in their original positions – several have been recut to give overly happy expressions. In 1820, when the church was reordered as we see it today the chancel arch was completely replaced. The south window of the

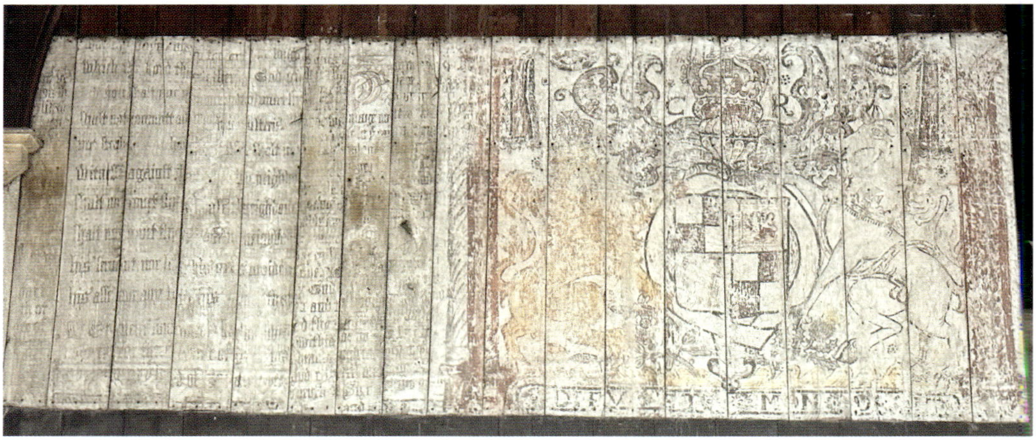

Haltham-on-Bain. The royal arms of Charles II and the Ten Commandments are painted on the planks forming the base of the tower.

chancel has its sill lowered to form a simple sedilia with a fourteenth-century angle piscina. In the centre of the chancel floor is a fine, though badly worn, ledger stone with an inscription in Lombardic lettering covering the grave of one of the Dymock lords of the manor. An overlooked feature of importance is the pair of iron rings set into the walls just above the Communion rails. These must have been installed pre-Reformation to support the Lenten veil, which hid the altar from view during the medieval period.

25. Halton Holegate, St Andrew

The fact that the chancel is roofed in slate is the only evidence you need that a major nineteenth-century campaign of repairs was undertaken. The work here was by local architect James Fowler, whose hand touched so many Lincolnshire churches and whose work deserves more credit. Not only did he rebuild the chancel but the tower as well and, between the two, reconstructed the nave. Yet the casual visitor might not notice this, so well was the task undertaken. On the south side we can see that the clerestory and porch are both built in smooth Ancaster stone ashlar, whilst the rest of the church is constructed of rough local greensand. Fowler added a band of Ancaster stone atop the tower to 'tie it in'. The porch really is magnificent with a frieze of deeply cut quatrefoils rising on the south side to a point over an image niche. A veritable gallery of smug faces surrounds the south door, although most have been recut. Our eyes are immediately drawn up to the medieval roof, where ten angels hover benignly on the congregation below. At the principal joins, painted bosses gleam, whilst each tie beam has a series of heads and foliate designs that are almost unseen. The spandrels supporting the tie beams are delicately carved. My favourite boss shows a deer, its jaws around the neck of a bird of prey. The church contains some lovely wooden bench ends, and the patina of centuries will show which are Victorian and which are medieval. The medieval scenes include one which demonstrates the rivalry between stonemasons and

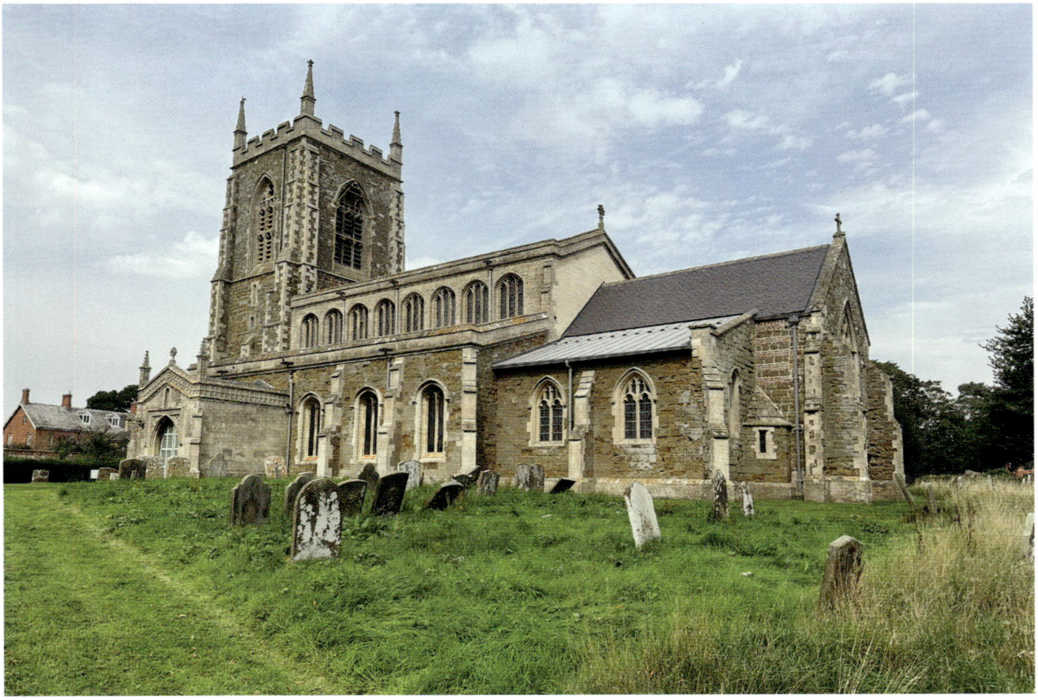

Above: Halton Holegate. The church stands on high ground. The contrast between the light Ancaster limestone and the darker greenstone of the rest of the church is easy to see.

Right: Halton Holegate. This fifteenth-century bench end depicts a stonemason accosted by another. Perhaps the woodcarver was having a dig at fellow workmen?

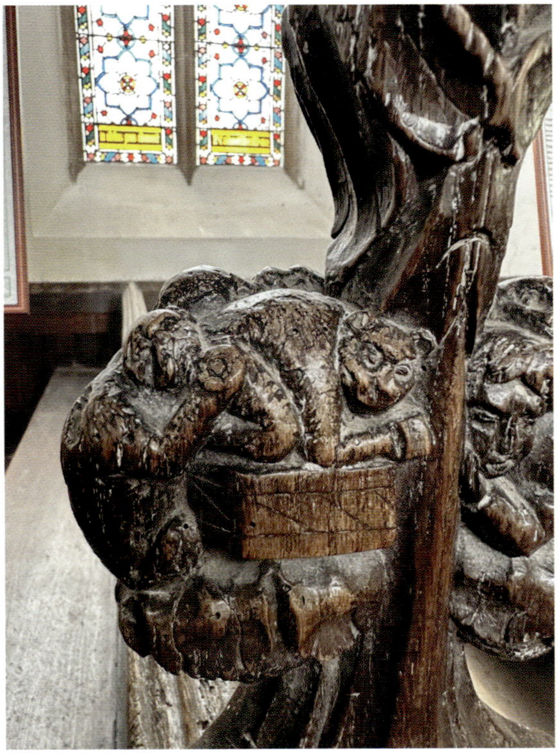

carpenters for it depicts masons as cats licking each other's bottoms! At the back of the church is a magnificent woollen model of the nearby church of Sutterby, which is now redundant and cared for by the Friends of Friendless Churches. It was made as part of a community project and is an accurate representation of the church; it is well worth a visit. One monument of note survives in the south aisle: a cross-legged knight of around 1320. He has a superb rampant lion on his shield, but unfortunately this is not enough to identify him.

26. Hannah cum Hagnaby, St Andrew

This simplest of churches, built in 1753, contains a well-preserved Georgian interior with box pews, a two-decker pulpit and a couple of surprises. The church is a simple rectangle with a west porch, roofed under a single structure covered with pantiles and a small bellcote. The interior is made up of wooden box pews painted to look like oak. The graining is particularly easy to see where light reflects off the doors. In the 1851 Census of Religious Worship, we learn that there were free seats for forty and rented seats for seventy. This was more than enough provision as the congregation numbered just twenty-five. For this reason, the church escaped Victorian restoration when so many ripped out pews in favour of

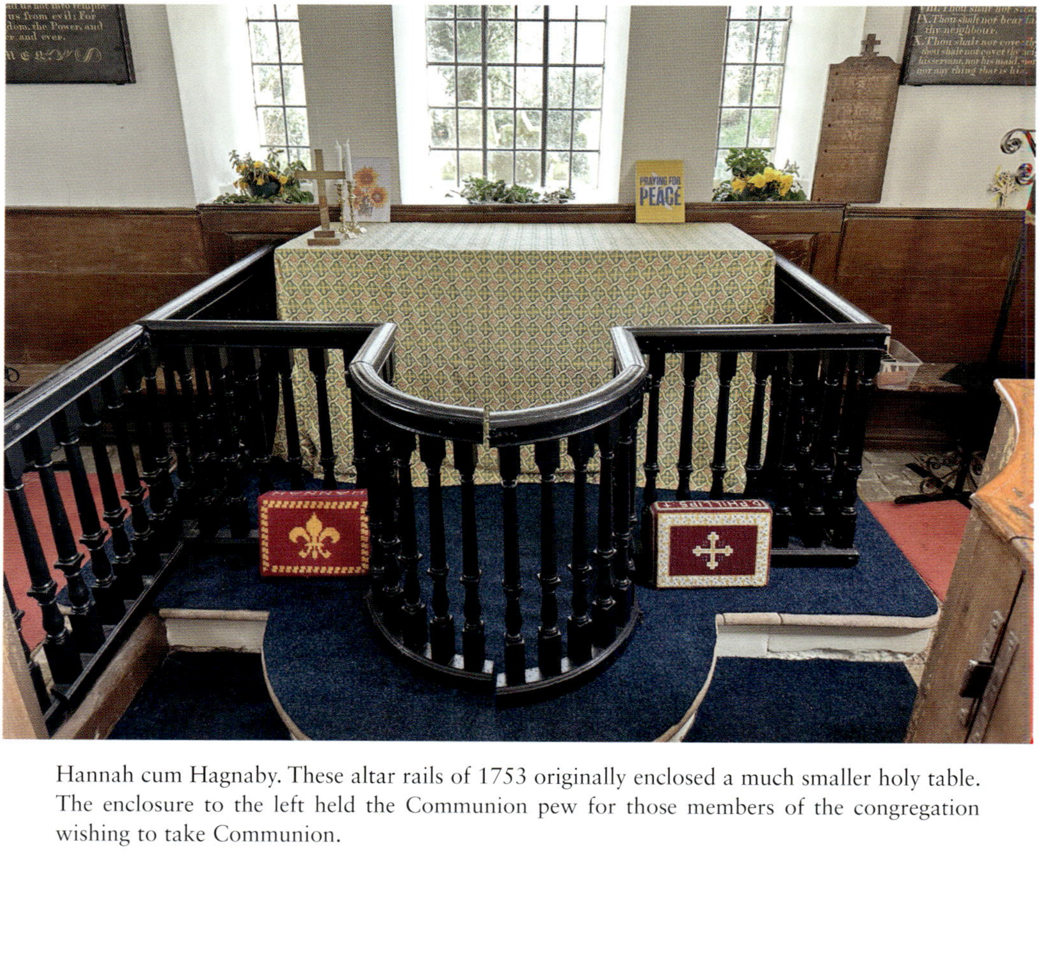

Hannah cum Hagnaby. These altar rails of 1753 originally enclosed a much smaller holy table. The enclosure to the left held the Communion pew for those members of the congregation wishing to take Communion.

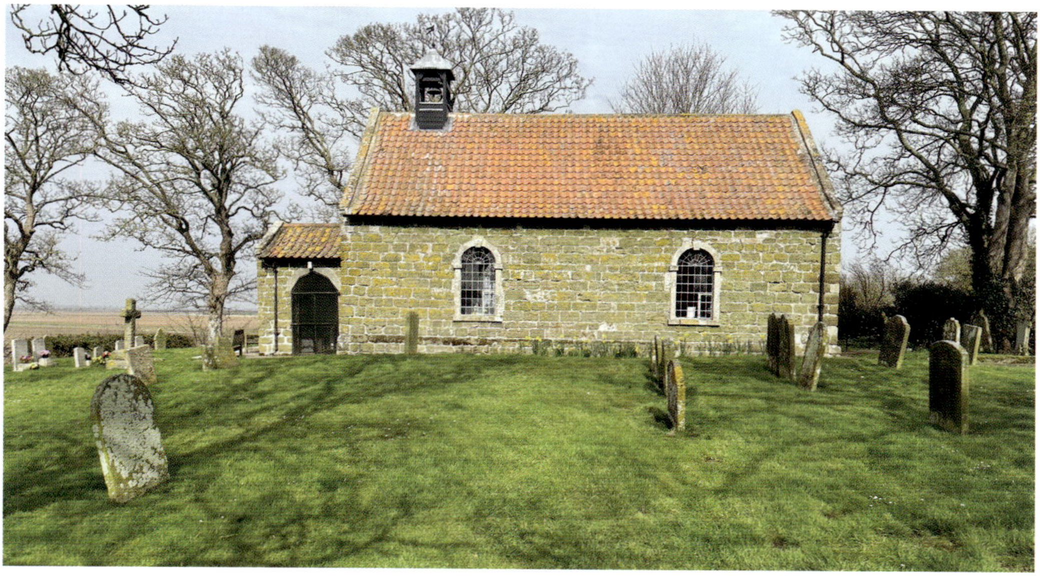

Hannah cum Hagnaby. Exterior from the south showing the way in which the greenstone was cut into large blocks for ease of construction. The pantile roof is typical of eastern counties of England, as the tiles were originally imported from the Low Countries.

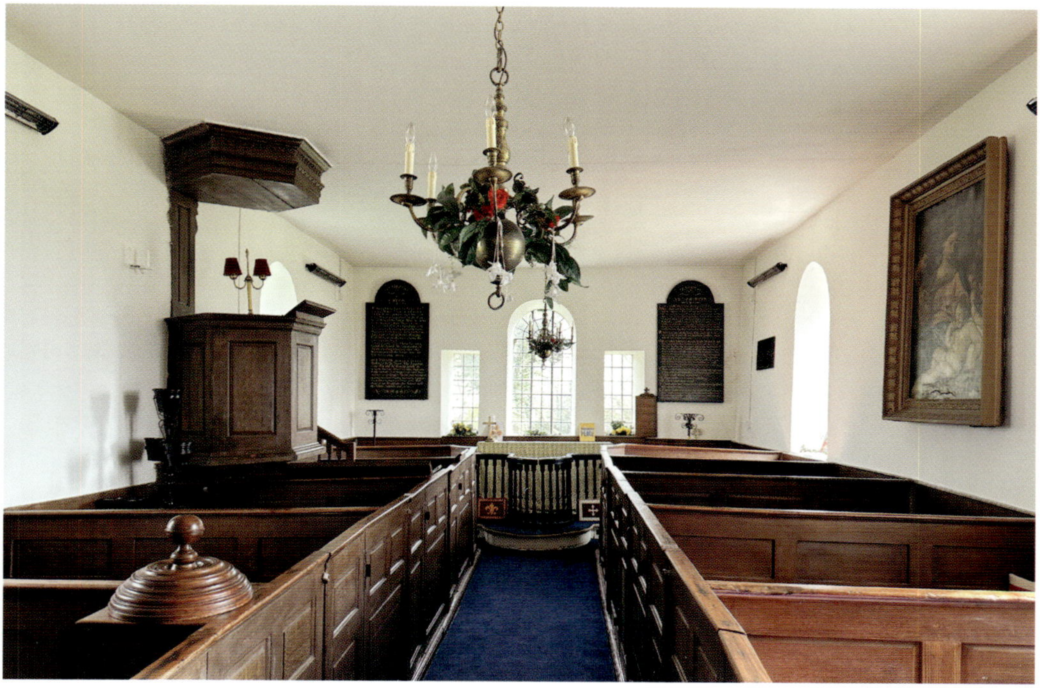

Hannah cum Hagnaby. Interior looking east, showing the pulpit halfway down the north wall. On the left is the tiny font built into its own pew. The Ten Commandments, Creed and Lord's Prayer on the east wall were required by law to be in that position in all Anglican churches at the time.

benches. The first surprise is the tiny marble font set under a circular finial cover, built into the rear pew on the north side. The graining of its case is especially fine. Nearby is the tall two-decker pulpit, which reaches right to the plaster ceiling. It stands in the traditional location for its date, dominating the entire interior. There is no stained glass, and the Creed and Ten Commandments hang either side of the east window – required by law in the Georgian period. Surprise number two is the set of altar rails with turned balusters. The centre section protrudes in a semicircle to allow the clergyman space to stand and bless the congregation. The rails are so close to the east wall there was insufficient space in front of the holy table, even though the original table would have been considerably smaller than the one in the church today. Importantly, on the north side of the church the rails extend to east and west to create a pew for those planning to receive Communion. Morning Prayer was the standard Sunday service and afterwards most of the congregation would go home, but on those rare occasions when Communion was held those staying would gather in this special pew near the altar. They survive in only a few churches. A third surprise at Hannah Church may be found in the porch on the way out where, either side of the door, are fragments of fifteenth-century carvings representing Apostles – St Andrew with his cross is especially easy to identify. They may have come from a doorway, or possibly a monument, in the previous building.

27. Ingoldmells, St Peter and St Paul

This lovely church is proof that there was great wealth here in the thirteenth century, which sadly did not continue for long. From the south it is obvious that the stone here was used in two different techniques. The tower and south aisle are of ashlar, the stone cut into regular blocks, whereas the clerestory is of stone rubble, the pieces unsquared and built into the wall in a higgledy-piggledy fashion. No doubt this was originally disguised by lime plaster. A palm tree shelters against the south wall. From the south it is obvious that a chancel has disappeared. It was demolished in the seventeenth century when its maintenance became too much of a drain – a similar scenario was followed at other local churches. Inside, the overwhelming feature is the large east wall where the chancel arch formerly stood. When the wall was constructed in the early eighteenth century it had a small round-headed window – the outline may just be picked out – but this probably became too expensive to maintain in such an exposed location and was subsequently blocked up. The arcades are typically of about 1200, their capitals differing as new ideas were embraced. Those carved with stiff leaf design are as good as any in the county, reflecting the work of stonemasons who had worked on more prestigious buildings. The highlight of a visit here, however, is a small memorial brass in the north chapel. The casual visitor might easily miss it, but here is a rare representation of a disabled man, William Palmer, who died in 1520. He is pictured with a crutch, or 'stylt' as the inscription says. At the back of the church is a huge grotesque, which once must have dominated the outside of the building. It has boggle eyes, an open mouth and clawed feet and would have been placed so as to frighten evil spirits away from the church.

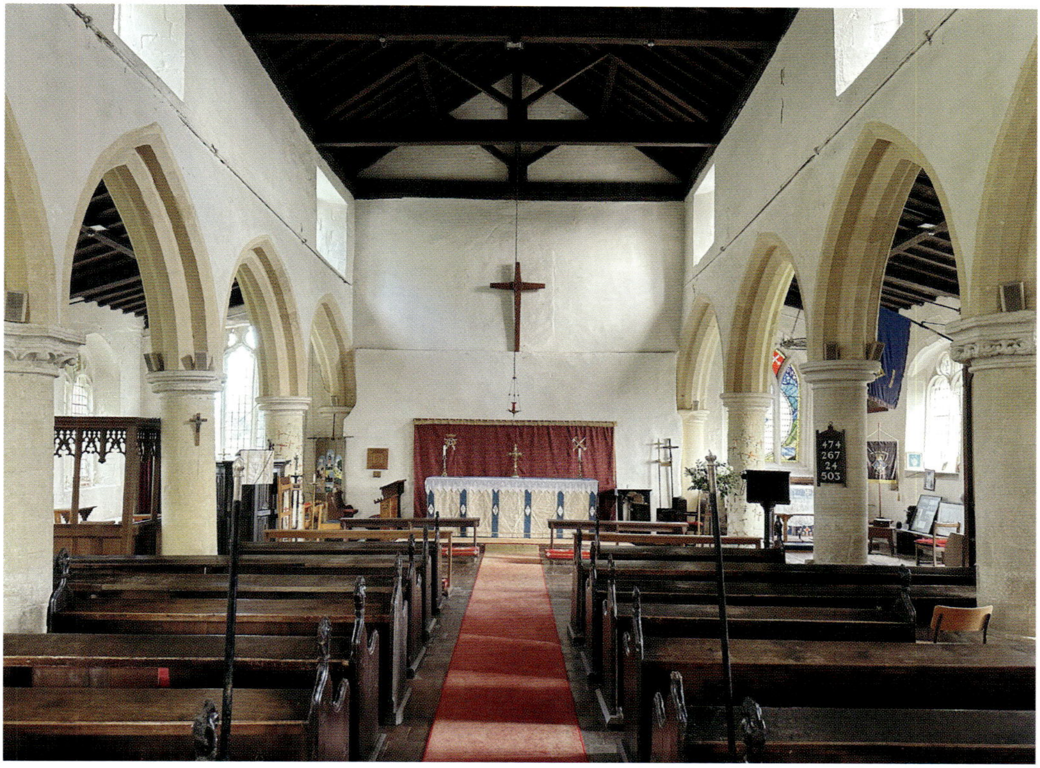

Above: Ingoldmells. The nave looking east towards the former chancel which was demolished in the seventeenth century when its maintenance became too much. The arcades date from the late twelfth century and just predate the Gothic period.

Right: Ingoldmells. The rare memorial brass to William Palmer (d. 1520), who is depicted with his crutch. His disability is mentioned in the inscription, which says: 'Pray for the soule of William Palmer with his stylt.'

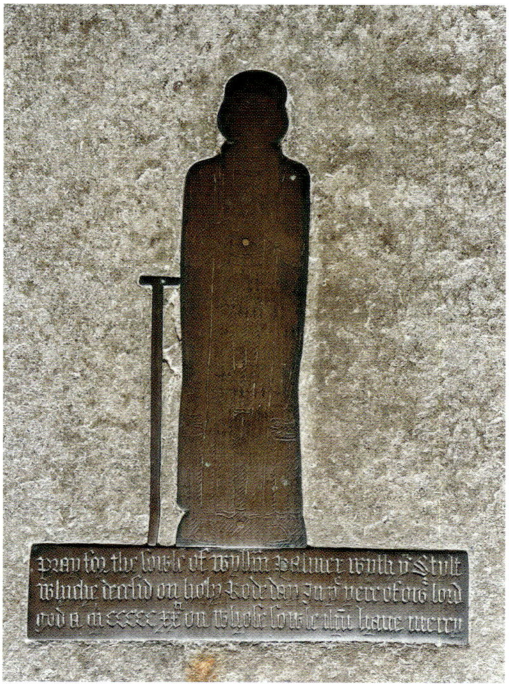

28. Ingoldsby, St Bartholomew

Set on high ground above the village street, the church consists of aisle, nave, chancel and low west tower. Inside the porch is an unforgettable fifteenth-century door with a former wicket. You can see the rusty marks left by nails over the centuries as official notices have been displayed on it. There are steps down into the church, which is flooded with light from the clerestory windows in the south wall. Unusually, there are no matching windows on the north side. The south arcade is fourteenth century with moulded arches – it may have been paid for by the person who was originally buried in the arched recess in the south aisle wall. However, the north aisle is Romanesque and dates from the late Norman period. The easternmost capital, above the pulpit, has been cut away – no doubt to take the rood screen and loft that would have run across the church at this point. The soft stone of which the church is built has been popular with graffiti artists over the centuries. Some is medieval, but most dates from the eighteenth century, especially under the tower. On a south pier of the nave is an interesting example, for in the Georgian period the church would have been filled with privately owned box pews and William Muston must have been especially proud of his as he carved into the wall 'W M Muston. His seat. July ye 19th 1710'. In the chancel is another fourteenth-century tomb recess, but the floor level at the east end of the church has been raised so that two steps now encroach on the scene. To the left of the recess is a half-arch from a former doorway, which shows that the chancel has been reduced in length in either the eighteenth or nineteenth century. Two

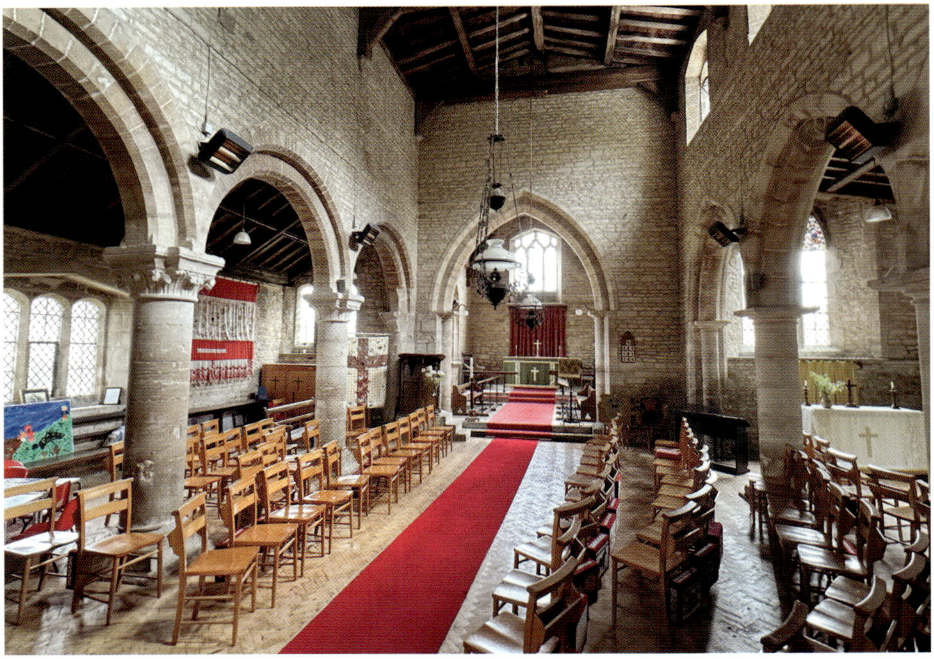

Ingoldsby. Interior looking east. Unusually, there are only clerestory windows on the south side. The capital has been cut away above the pulpit to give room for access to the rood loft that once crossed the arch.

chairs with interesting carved panels were probably carved in the Netherlands. Hanging in the north aisle is a rare survival: a banner of the Order of Oddfellows. Painted in the reign of Queen Victoria, it was later changed to read 'God Save the King'. The society had a branch in the village and even its own hall. Thanks to a churchwarden here the banner was saved when the branch was closed.

29. Kingerby, St Peter

A diminutive church sitting on the bend of the road in a tidy churchyard. The south wall of the chancel displays a low side window. It was once believed that these were used by lepers, but the preferred explanation today is that they were for ventilation of the chancel and to create a bit of church theatre by causing the candles to flicker. Inside the porch, the Romanesque doorway of the twelfth century reminds us of the early origins of the church. The two stone benches there were used by witnesses to weddings and legal transactions. Inside, the ogee-headed arch to the tower and the octagonal font both point to a fourteenth-century renovation, as does the glass in the south aisle. Here we find images of St Catherine (clearly holding her wheel) and St Cecilia holding a portable organ. Surprisingly, the image of St Cecilia is Victorian, convincingly copying the style of the Catherine image. High in the west wall is a circular window which now leads into the tower. It is probably Saxon in date, just before the Norman Conquest, and

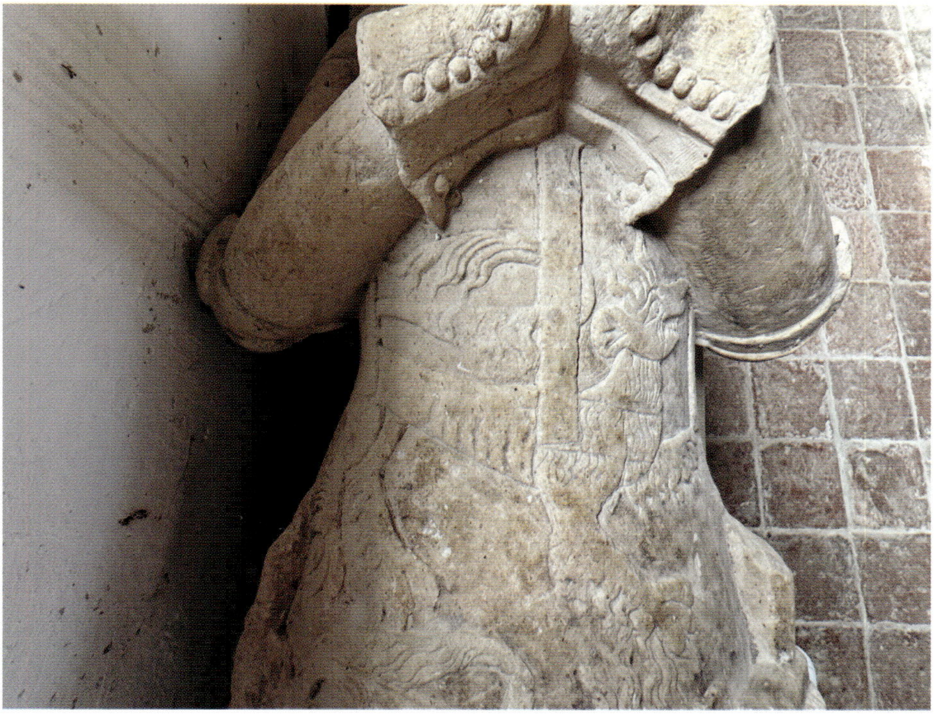

Kingerby. The elaborately carved armour on the effigy of a member of the Disney family includes a lion rampant on his surcoat.

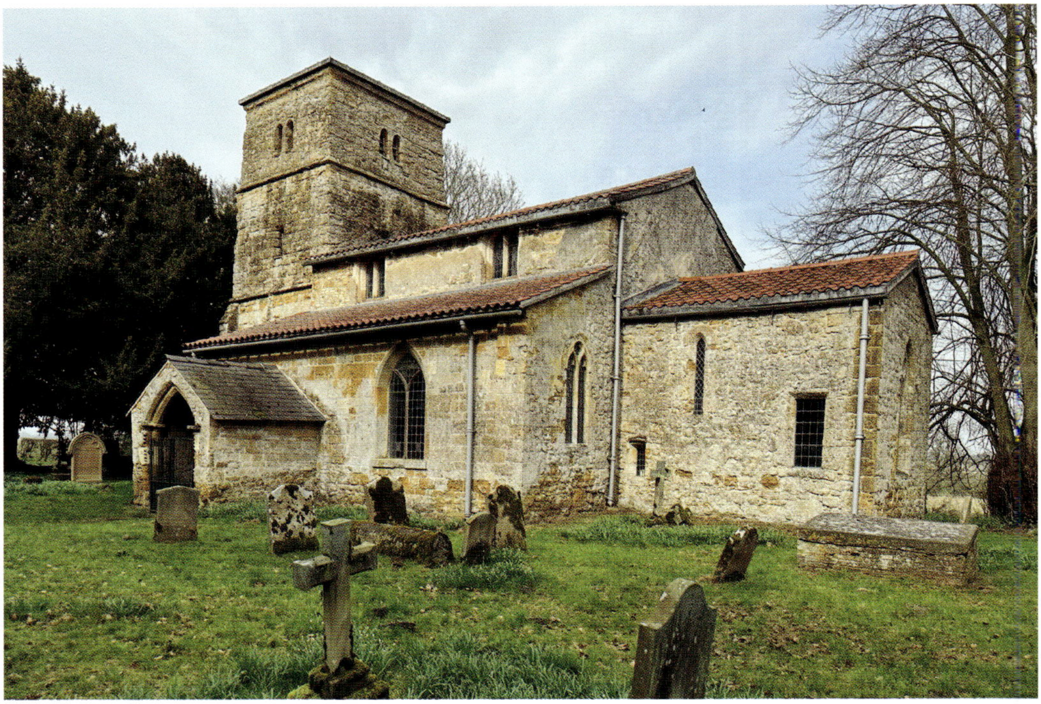

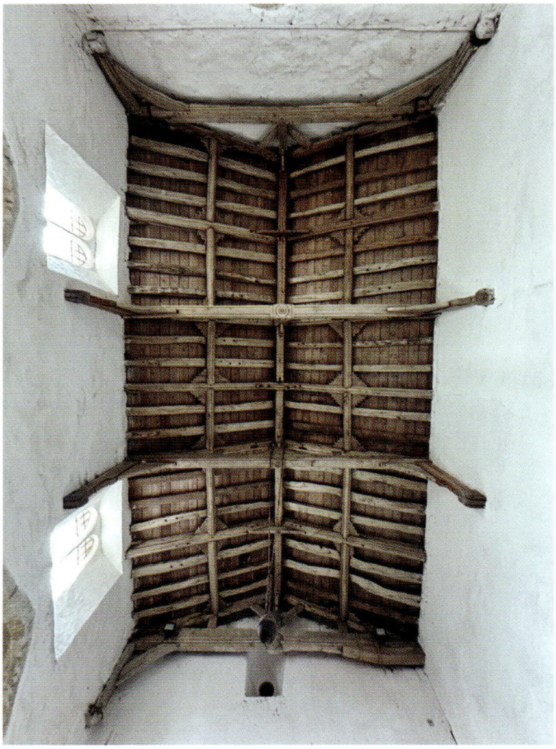

Above: Kingerby. In this view we see a tiny window in the south chancel wall. This is a low side window which we now believe was there to create a draught of air to create medieval theatre by causing the lamps on the rood screen to flicker.

Left: Kingerby. Missed by many is this charming three-bay, seventeenth-century roof.

would have lit the church before the tower was built. The stone tracery of the nave windows is also fourteenth century, the large north nave window dating from about 1300. There are three fine memorials to discover. The earliest is a coffin lid now displayed on its side in the chancel which takes the form of a demi-effigy (although he still shows feet at the bottom). The floriate arch over his head dates it to the mid-fourteenth century. In the south aisle are two effigies of roughly the same date. One has an impressive lion on his surcoat; the other has charming dogs at his shoulders. All three monuments are to members of the Disney family, lords of the manor here, although their main estate was at Norton Disney. The monuments originally stood in a long-demolished north aisle, one pier of which has been exposed behind the pulpit. A little-noticed but important feature of the nave is its three-bay roof, an addition of the early seventeenth century.

30. Kirmington, St Helen

The tall copper spire atop its ironstone tower draws us towards a church which certainly deserves more visitors. Though frequently dismissed because of the harsh restoration carried out by S. S. Teulon in 1859, there is actually far more of interest to be discovered here. Teulon definitely had his work cut out as the church he was charged with repairing had been patched up on more than one occasion. Its fourteenth-century north aisle had been demolished and the arcade filled in. This is where we must give Teulon praise, as he reopened it to create a very narrow north aisle, specifically to allow us to appreciate the magnificent figurative

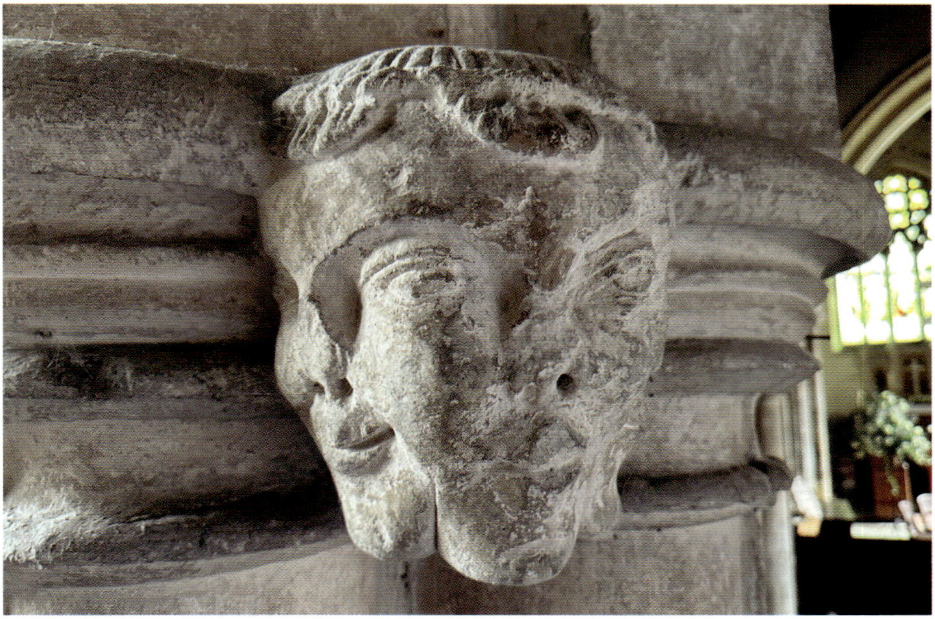

Kirmington. This carving on a nave capital depicts a three-faced figure, not uncommonly found in churches. Whilst the jury is still out on why it is incorporated in a church, the best guess is that it represents the past, present and future.

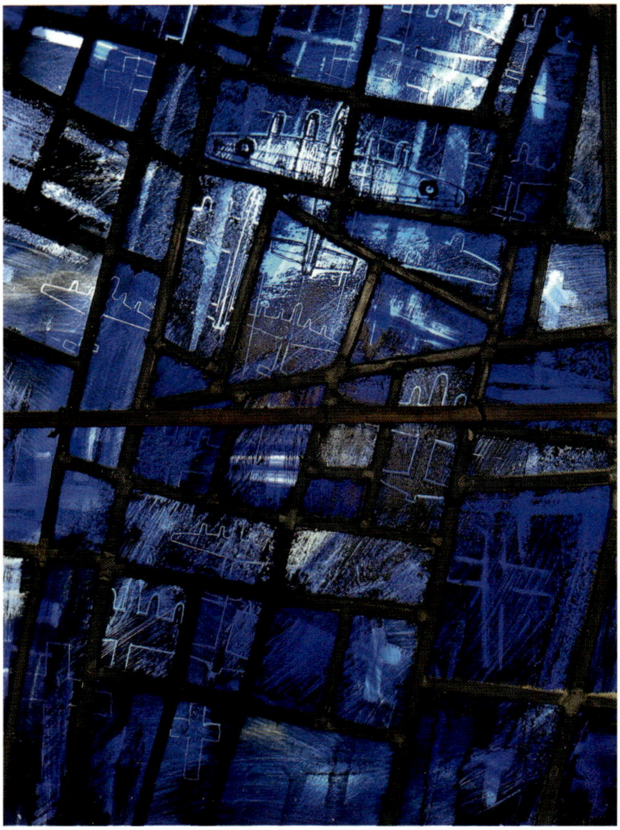

Kirmington. A detail of the window by Glenn Carter (1991) which commemorates 166 RAF Squadron of RAF Kirmington.

carving on its capitals. There are images of Synagoga wearing a blindfold; a bishop with his hand raised in blessing; an angry man with hollowed-out eyes; and, best of all, an image of the three-faced head. The jury is still out on what it means. A common theory is that it represents the Holy Trinity, but there are plenty of more conventional images of that scene in our churches. I prefer to think of it as a form of Janus figure, its faces looking backwards and forwards in time. This is a subject often associated with doorways, and this capital is right where the original north door to the church would have been. The arcade on the south side is much more pedestrian with octagonal piers and plain capitals, perhaps a couple of generations after the north arcades. They were preserved by Teulon, but the chancel arch was not so lucky, and the contrast in texture of the stone is clear to see. The nominally Gothic reredos with its sacred monogram and inset marble cross is raised above the ordinary by its superb marble gradine shelf, whilst two stained-glass windows attract our attention. On the north wall of the chancel is a modern window to commemorate 166 RAF Squadron of RAF Kirmington, based at what is now Humberside Airport. Its deep blue multi-panes contain the outline of Lancaster Bombers. The artist was Glenn Carter (1991). In the north aisle is an odd window in grisaille design, like a traditional stained-glass cartoon, depicting the vision on the road to Damascus and Christ sending out the Apostles.

31. Langton by Spilsby, St Peter and St Paul

Very much a church from the time of Jane Austen, it was built in the 1720s and is little changed from its Georgian form. It stands on a hillock and is built of red brick, which forms a single rectangular space. Surprisingly, there are no windows in the east wall, just a series of recesses to make the wall less severe. The low-pitched roof hangs over the walls in deep eaves and an octagonal bell turret rises above the west end. It is both curious and endearing. The interior is one of the finest Georgian interiors to survive, although, like most churches, things have been moved about over the years. The first thing that strikes you is a bust of Revd Charles Langton, three times married into early nineteenth-century families of note, including Wedgwood and Darwin. As you enter under the west gallery the quality of woodwork throughout the church is obvious. The two fluted columns of the gallery frame an interior of box pews, three-decker pulpit and reredos. The pews closest to the holy table are curved inwards to create an architectural division between nave and sanctuary and the font, which must have come from an earlier church; the table stands at the east end, where it did in many churches of this period. The Communion rails with turned spindles close together to keep the area around the table separate and surround it on three sides. The panelling on the

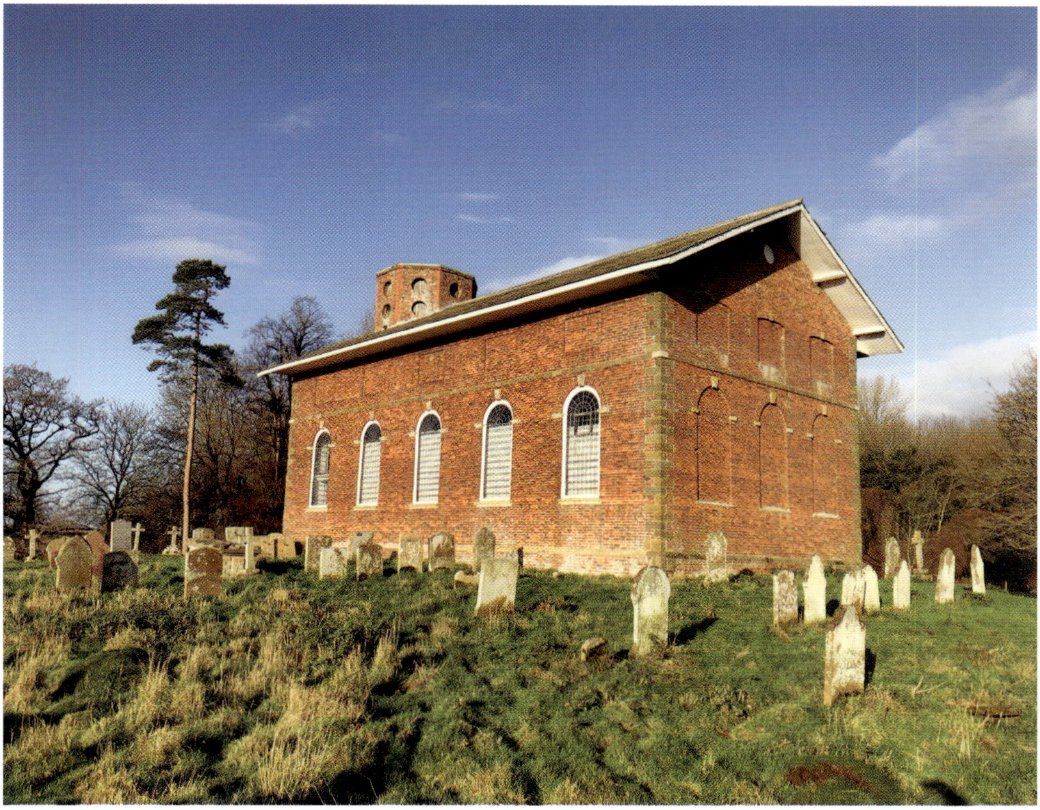

Langton by Spilsby. A red-brick, single-cell church of the 1720s was given its octagonal bell turret 100 years later.

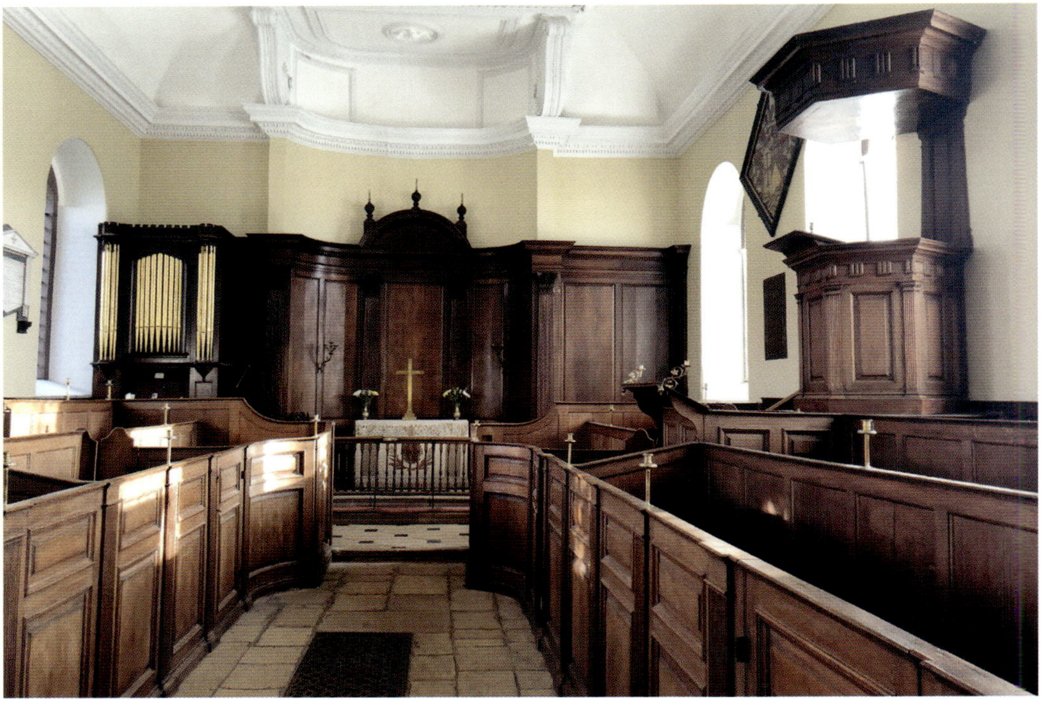

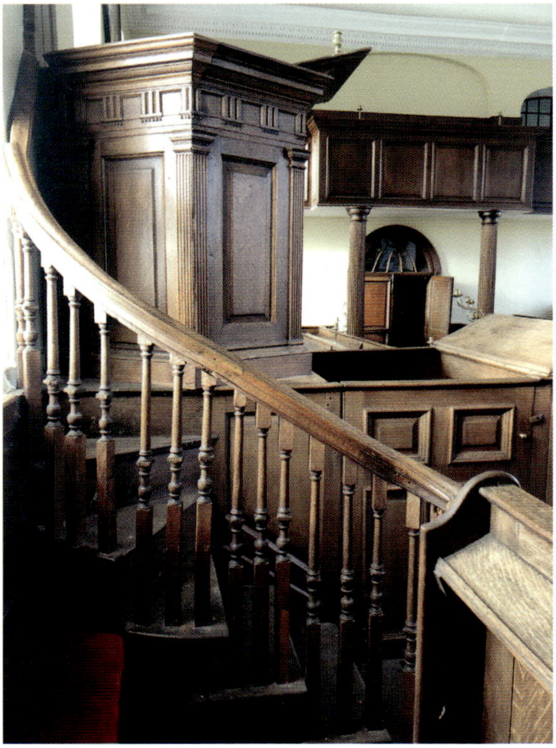

Above: Langton by Spilsby. Interior looking east, showing the box pews of varying heights and sizes which would have ensured the class segregation in daily life was also replicated in the house of God.

Left: Langton by Spilsby. Of all the details in this remarkable church, the curving handrail leading to the three-decker pulpit is good honest work by a village carpenter.

east wall must once have been painted with the Creed, Ten Commandments and Lord's Prayer as required by law at the time, but I rather prefer the way in which it now blends with everything else. There are four memorial hatchments, the most recent of which is only twenty years old. The most complex design – and one of the most complex in the county – is that where the back is divided into four black-and-white stripes and commemorates Bennett Langton. He married a dowager countess whose coronet can be seen in the right-hand half. At the west end of the nave are two ledger stones to members of the Langton family which came from the previous church, whilst in the porch is a stone sculpture of the Crucifixion which dates from the thirteenth century.

32. LOUTH, ST JAMES

Lincolnshire's urban churches are amongst the finest of any English county. This was a wealthy part of England in the late medieval period, with only neighbouring Norfolk surpassing it. Whilst the rural churches can also display extraordinary wealth it is in the urban setting where guilds and multiple chantries provided added sources of income and where the finest churches are found. At Louth it is all about the exterior. The tower and spire were built over a period of about seventy-five years, starting in 1440. Luckily, building accounts survive which give us the names of masons involved – John Scule, Lawrence Lemyng and John Tempas. It is quite

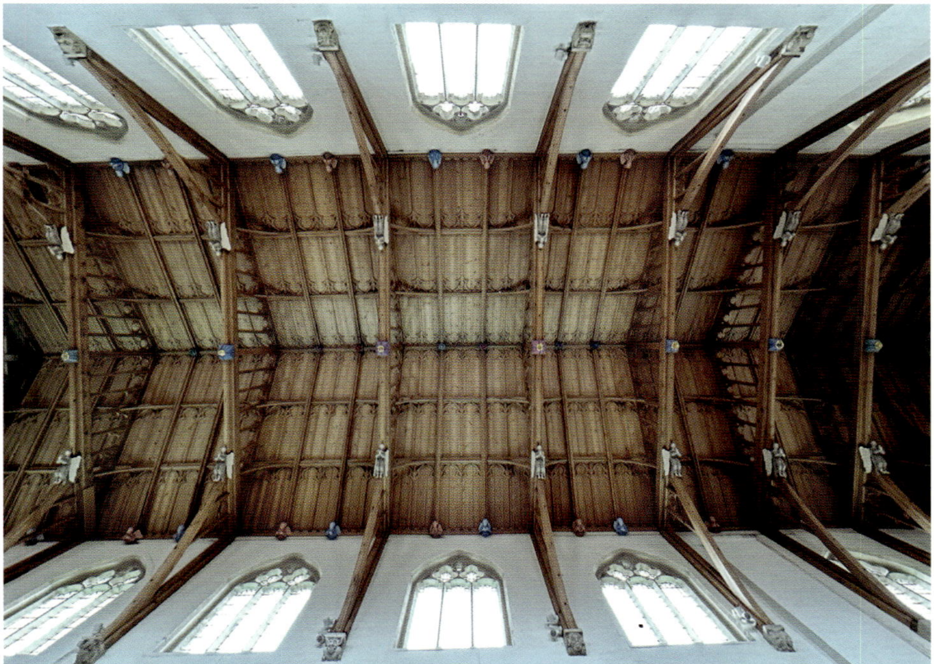

Louth. This huge urban church was given a new roof in 1825 in the then fashionable Gothic style, where the pointed arch was all about appearance rather than structure.

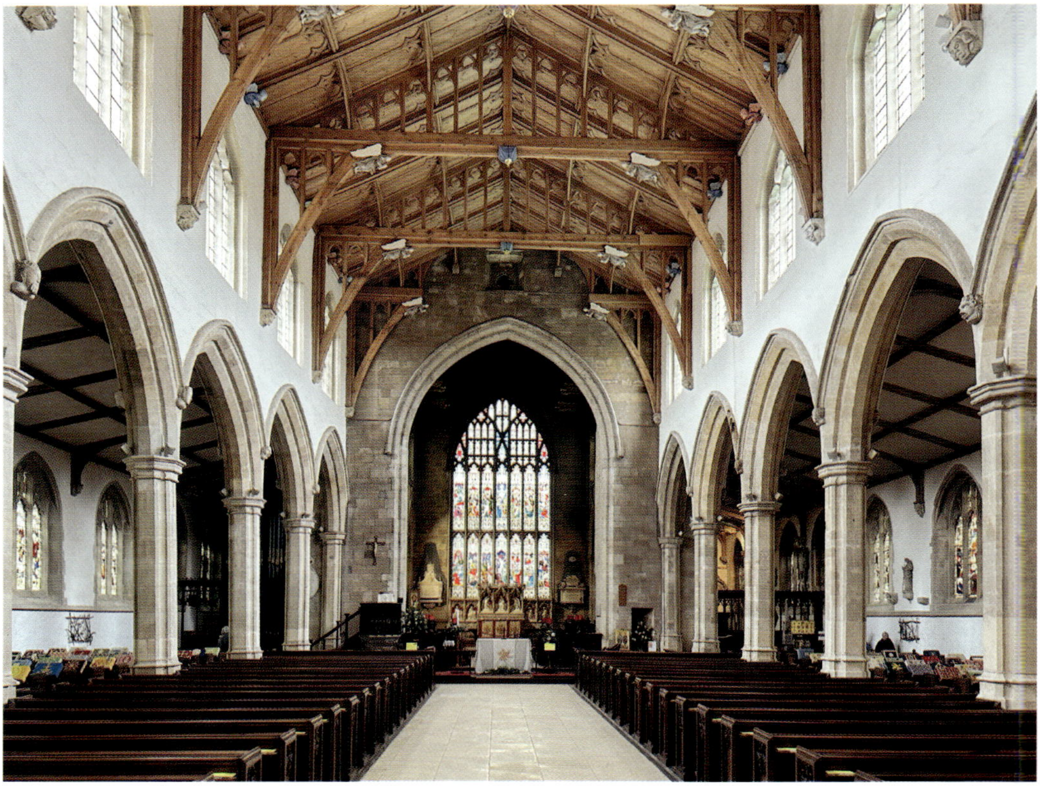

Louth. Interior looking east, showing the width of the church with its aisles and the uniform benches added by James Fowler, the diocesan architect, in the 1860s.

something to be able to credit named individuals with something that still stands after 500 years. The west door is original and at the top are two shields which must have once borne the donor's names. The right-hand shield is delightful as it is being held by a tiny hand, whilst its partner is just hanging from a nail. As usual, the interior is a result of nineteenth-century restoration when post-Reformation accretions were removed, including box pews and galleries. Today the interior is enhanced at the west end by a café, storage rooms and notice boards designed by the late Richard Benny. The arcades are a novel design with a recessed moulding on four of its eight sides. Some people have suggested that these are recut piers from an earlier church, and there is some evidence that this may be correct as the windows don't line up with the arcades as we would normally expect. The original roof must have been very fine for there are two statues in the chapel behind the organ which once graced the nave, each holding a symbol of Christ's Passion. They are similar to those still in the church at Burwell (see entry 10). The present roof is in rather spindly Georgian Gothic and dates from 1825. The Victorian architect responsible for the church as we see it today was James Fowler (1828–92), whose practice was based in the town. In the south chapel is a memorial bust of him looking very much the local statesman (he was mayor of Louth five times).

33. Navenby, St Peter

Proudly sitting on the edge of the escarpment away from the bustling high street, its leafy churchyard exhibits many examples of headstones with a single hole drilled through. This is very much a Lincolnshire tradition, where an upright wooden post was sunk into the ground and used to support the headstone from behind, to which it was attached via the hole. Most posts have rotted away, leaving the visitor from

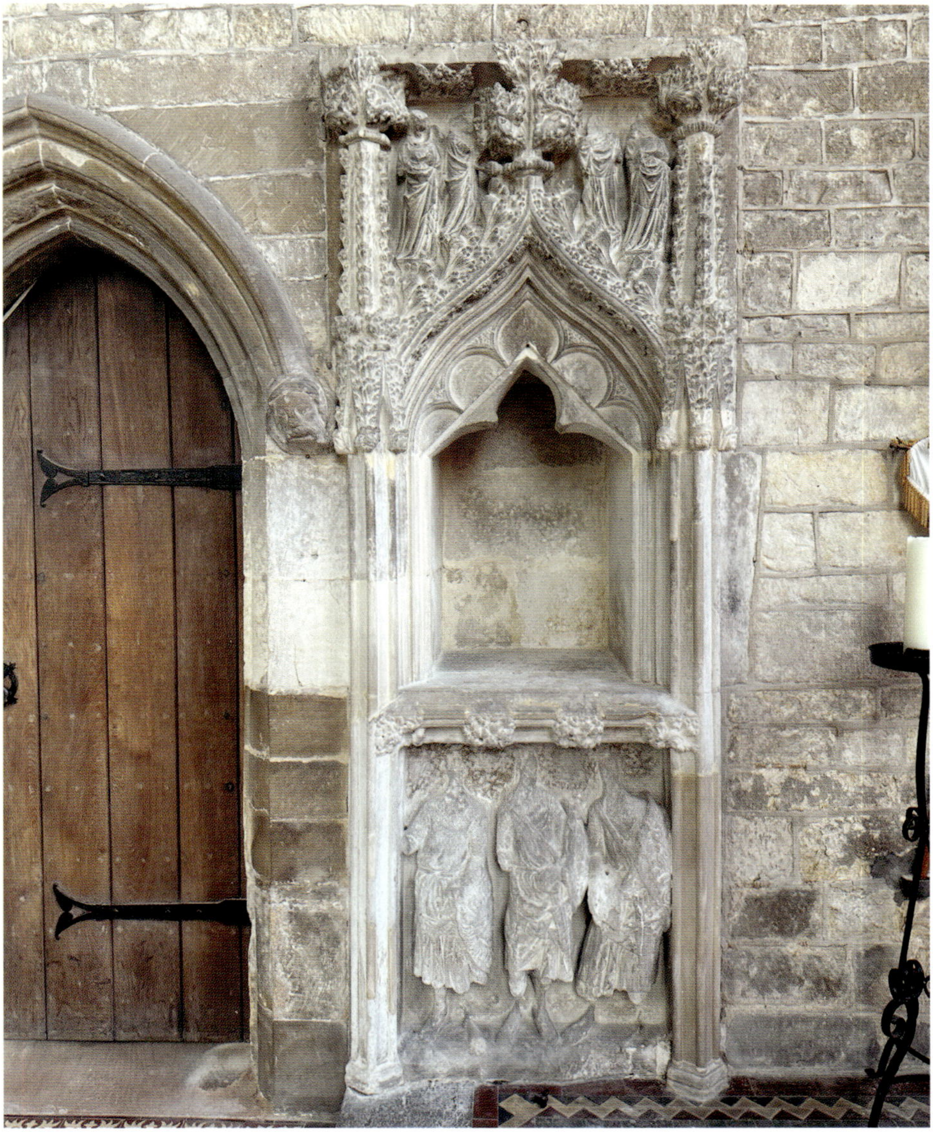

Navenby. Fourteenth-century housing for the Easter Sepulchre, where a consecrated wafer served as a focus of devotion as part of the Easter weekend. At the base are the soldiers who were supposed to guard Christ's body, whilst at the top are the three Marys and the angel that told them he had gone.

other parts to puzzle over such an odd feature. The church is another display of fourteenth-century bravado, sculpture being the order of the day wherever you look, with gargoyles, grotesques and friezes. In the south aisle there is a good example of a musician with pipe and tabor – often placed high up to scare evil spirits out of the roof. The nave is large and light with the view being dominated at the east end by a twentieth-century screen with rood above designed by Temple Moore. The loft sits on a surviving medieval bracket and lines up with the upper door, so it is certain that its proportions mirror what was there before the Reformation. Above, you can see the earlier roof line, from before the clerestory windows were added. At the back of the church the base of the tower is now a rich baptistry with red-and-green stencilled walls and a font of 1862. It is in stark contrast to the scraped walls of the rest of the church. Above the tower arch is a large royal arms from the reign of Queen Anne with her personal motto 'Semper Eadem'. The artist, Thomas Hunton, has signed his name prominently at the bottom with the year '1710'. The chancel contains most medieval treasures. On the north side is a tomb recess that would have marked the burial place of whoever paid for the rebuilding of the chancel in the early fourteenth century. Further along is a splendid Easter sepulchre, a niche in which the consecrated host would have been displayed over the days prior to the first Mass of Easter. At the base are three soldiers, representing the soldiers whose job was to guard the tomb of Jesus. Above are four smaller figures which represent the three Marys who went to the tomb and the angel who told them that Jesus was no longer there. The angel is second from the left, their wings just visible, swinging a thurible into the foliage. Opposite the Easter sepulchre is the sedilia made useless by a later raising of the floor. It was obviously designed as a set with the sepulchre and tomb recess, and whilst it might be tempting to add the double piscina to the set it is obviously a generation or two earlier.

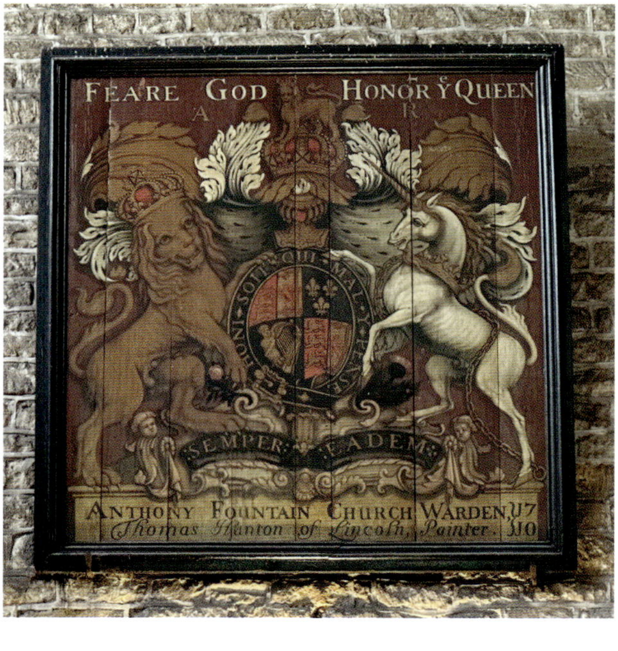

Navenby. This royal arms is of Queen Anne (1702–14) and painted on wooden boards. It bears her personal motto, 'Semper Eadem', which translates as 'Always the same'. It also records the name of the churchwarden who commissioned it together with that of the painter.

34. Normanby le Wold, St Peter

Known to the many walkers on the Wolds, St Peter's is the highest church in Lincolnshire and stands in a delightful dead-end location. On the south side there is a blocked doorway dating from the thirteenth century – the earliest architectural feature to survive Fowler's restoration of 1867. This work included rebuilding the aisle and adding a new chancel and finally roofing the whole in slate. Next to the blocked doorway is an original window which may be compared to Fowler's replacements in a different stone. Inside, the new chancel arch and first arches of the arcade are Victorian using two different coloured stones in contrast. The westernmost piers of the arcade each have a most curious carving, which the guide describes as a 'trumpet curl'. It certainly demonstrates the skill of the stonemason in the fourteenth century, who was able to cut through the solid stone. Others have referred to it as a ram's horn or, as I prefer, a pig's tail. Of the same date is the octagonal font, no doubt saved by Fowler to be a direct link to the villagers in generations past. There's nothing like being able to point out that your ancestors have been baptised in the same font for centuries. Three large Victorian paintings on canvas are part of a set distributed amongst other local churches. At the west end of the south aisle, set into the floor, is a very worn demi-effigy of a woman. Sadly, she has no inscription, but as the carving dates from the 1320s it would be tempting to suggest that she paid for the font and arcades to be built. A little further down the south aisle is the feature everyone remembers from the church. A cross-arch creates a chapel at the east end of each aisle, and on the south side its corbel is boldly carved with a man being distracted by toothache. It's a scene depicted in many medieval churches, but this example is especially powerful. The church contains some fine oval panels of Continental glass, probably dating from the eighteenth century, and also a

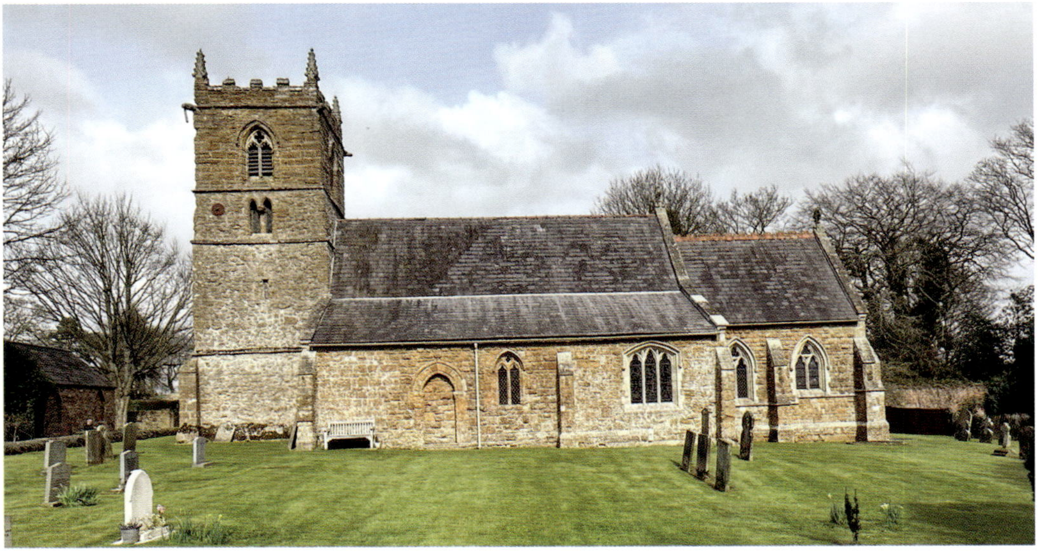

Normanby le Wold. This delightful church is much loved by walkers, who use it as a convenient place to rest. Despite a heavy Victorian restoration, it still retains much of interest.

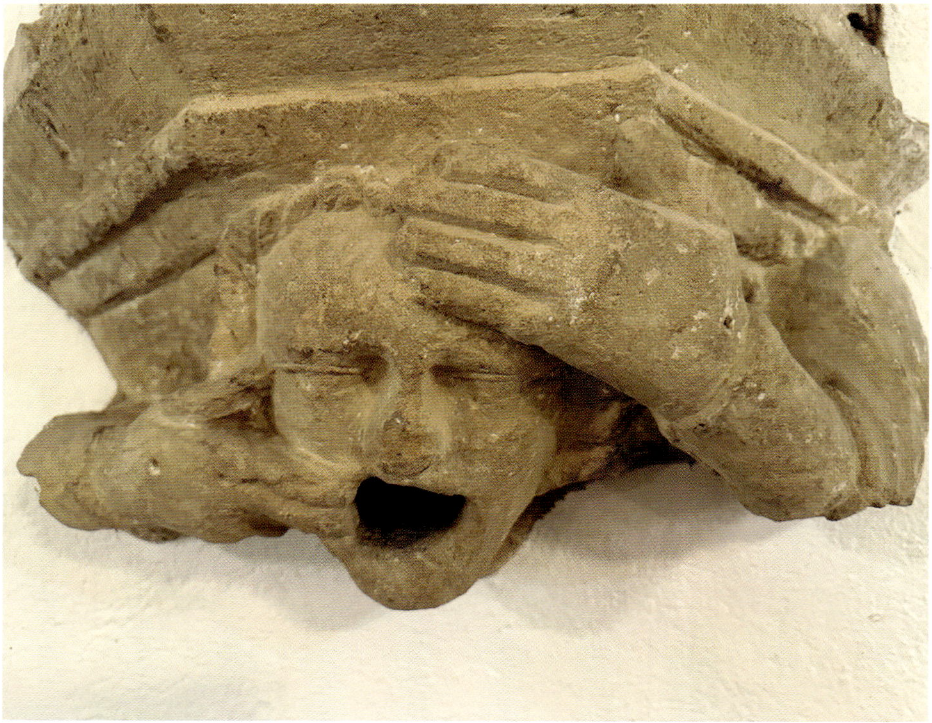

Normanby le Wold. A startlingly lifelike medieval carving of a man with toothache. It reminds us that the medieval church was just as much about the secular as it was the sacred.

detailed representation of the Annunciation by Kempe dating from 1907. Fowler's reredos, with two Germanic towers, incorporates not just a cross but the Alpha and Omega figures and is set off against a marble-lined east wall. On the sill of the easternmost window of the north aisle is an inlaid inscription recording the fact that the Hargrave family paid for the rebuilding of the north aisle in memory of their ancestors who worshipped here.

35. Oxcombe, All Saints

This charming out-of-the-way church is one of a small group of similar churches built on the cusp of the Victorian age. As such, they are not easy to categorise, being an amalgam of Georgian Gothic and embryonic Gothic Revival designs. Oxcombe is the tiniest, built on a slope below the farmyard of Oxcombe House. This in itself gives a clue as to what you're going to find, for both buildings were designed by the Lincoln-based architect W. A. Nicholson. The church is built of brick with stone dressings, the main architectural feature being an octagonal pinnacle lantern tower at the west end. The latter is of stone and stands out well against the brick, although no doubt the brick was originally covered in render to make it less obvious. The church has only five windows, each square headed and of two lights, which makes the interior rather dark, especially as the east

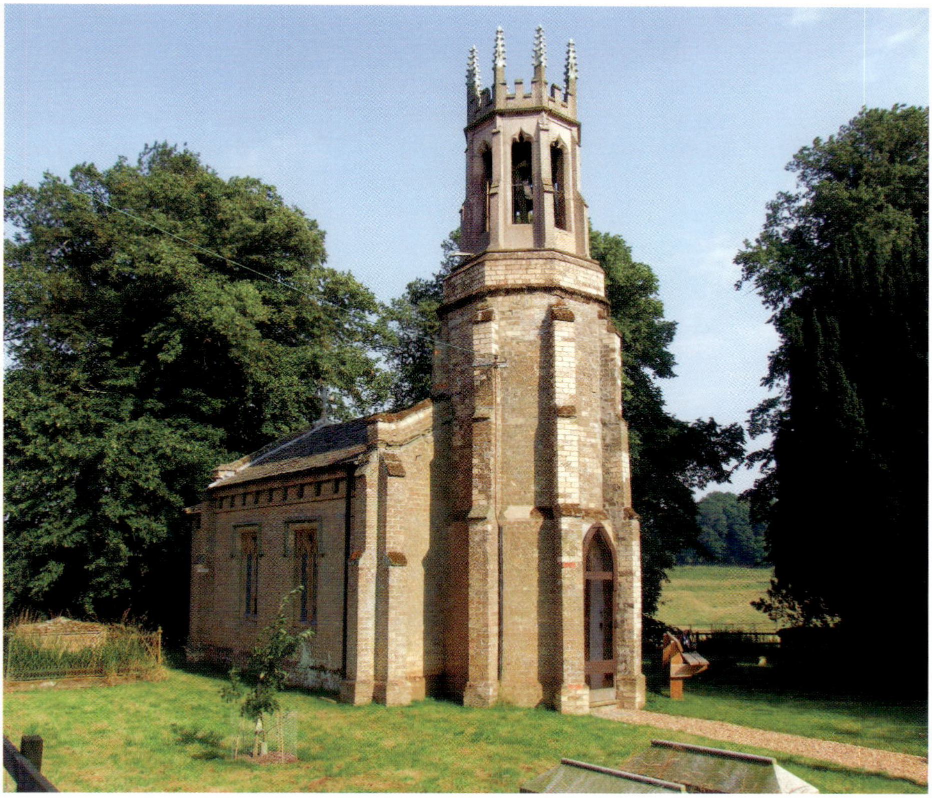

Oxcombe. This tiny early nineteenth-century church was designed in the Gothic style. Whilst it is built of brick, this would not originally have been seen as it was designed to be covered with Roman cement in imitation of stone. However, this caused the church to be damp and has been removed. (Image by Simon Knott)

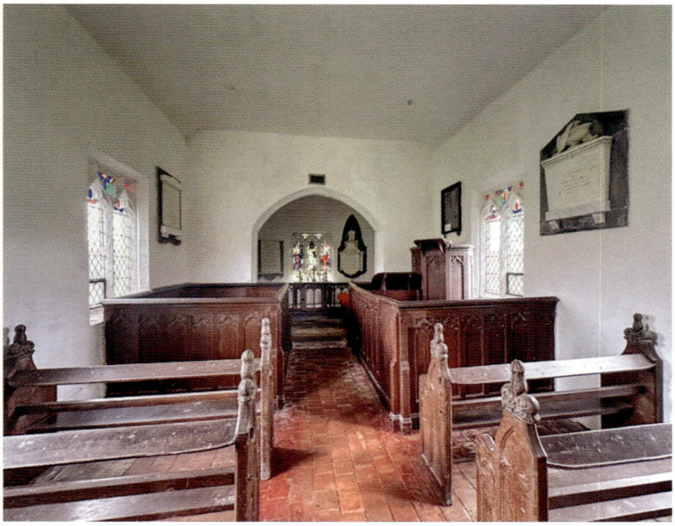

Oxcombe. The servants sat on open benches whilst the owners of the manor house and rectory had their own box pews. The glass in the nave windows is contemporary with the building, whilst the east window is a First World War memorial.

window has a scene in stained glass of the empty tomb installed by the lord of the manor, Sir Francis Sowerby Bennett, in memory of those from his estate who served in the First World War. It was designed by Heaton, Butler and Bayne and based on the painting *Easter Morning* by the Norwegian artist Axel Ender. A brass roll of honour records the names of thirteen men and one woman who left this idyllic fold in the Wolds. Ten returned. The four nave windows have brightly coloured glass designs in their tracery in the Georgian manner. The nave contains two large box pews with Gothic panelling for the house and rectory and open benches with poppyheads for the lower classes. The chancel is packed with tablets to the Grant family, some removed from the previous building. That to John Grant has a curious story. He was the patriarch of the family, purchasing the estate in 1789 and making a fortune. Originally this monument proudly displayed an inscription to the effect that he was the first man to make £100,000 from farming in Lincolnshire, but a descendant probably thinking this too vulgar had it chiselled off, which is why there is a large recessed blank rectangular area in the centre. The Grants sold off the estate after a few decades and it subsequently passed through a number of families.

36. Pickworth, St Andrew

Lincolnshire churches are proud of their stone spires, and they don't have to be elaborate to be effective. This is one of the plainer examples in what is known as the broach form, where the corners of the tower join the octagonal spire in little pyramid shapes. At the east end of the south aisle is a tiny circular turret which carried the rood loft stair. In the chancel south wall is a low side window for ventilation during Mass, and further east is a window with tracery of about 1300. Next to it is an inscription recording that the tomb chest below had a trust fund of 40*s* a year to maintain it 'for ever'. I wonder what happened! The visitor steps down through a medieval door with magnificent thirteenth-century hinges onto an uneven floor – evidence that the Victorians didn't spend too much money here. Consequently, the church has a terrific atmosphere, with layer upon layer of history visible. The church is seated with medieval benches and all around are remains of wall paintings. The most important are over the chancel arch, where we find a doom painting with souls rising from their graves and the lost heading towards the jaws of Hell (take binoculars). Elsewhere, the nave walls have a scheme of tiny flowers, although later scenes were painted over the top. On the north wall you can just pick out the three skeletons in the woods from the story of the Three Living and Three Dead. Over the top of these two medieval schemes, godly texts were added after the Reformation and even an inscription recalling repairs to the church in 1772. Between the nave and chancel is a rood screen that survived sixteenth-century destruction, although its loft is a modern replacement. Look at the tracery panels from the chancel side and you'll see that they are made from single panels of wood that are created by fretwork. On the south side of the chancel arch is the bottom of the staircase, which we saw outside, and above it is a defaced medieval saint. On the other side of the pier is an image bracket which still has red paint behind it to act as a background to another statue – now lost.

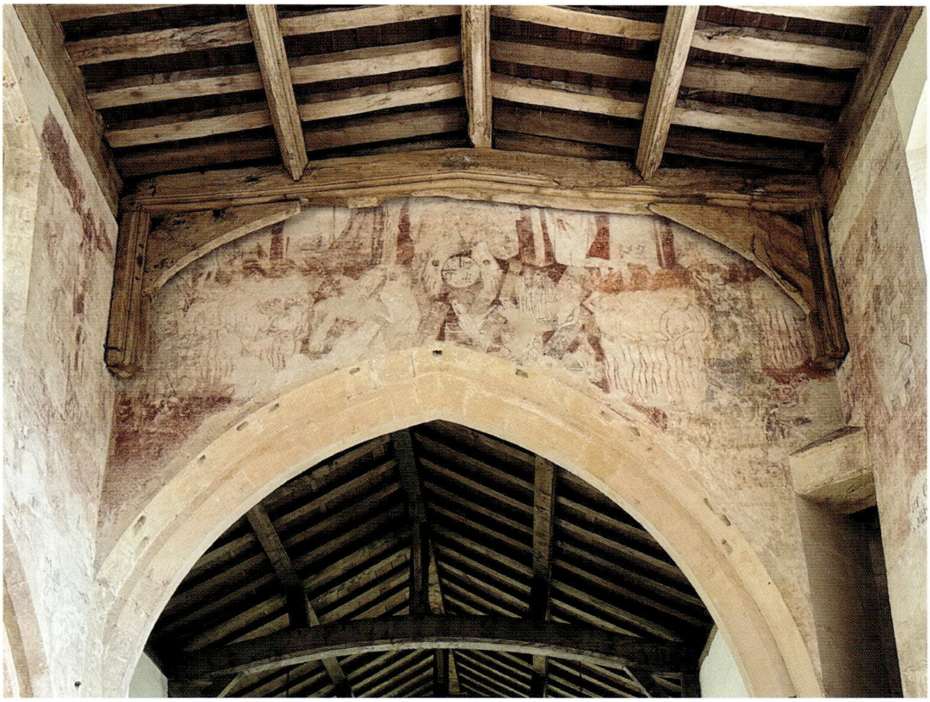

Above: Pickworth. An atmospheric church with some wonderful medieval wall paintings. Here is a version of the Doom, with souls climbing out of their graves on the left and the damned being consigned to Hell on the bottom right. The notches in the arch originally held a wooden tympanum against which stood the rood.

Right: Pickworth. The thirteenth-century door retains its original ironwork designed to hold the five vertical planks of wood together. The dark dots in the top third are rusty nails which, over the centuries, have held official notices.

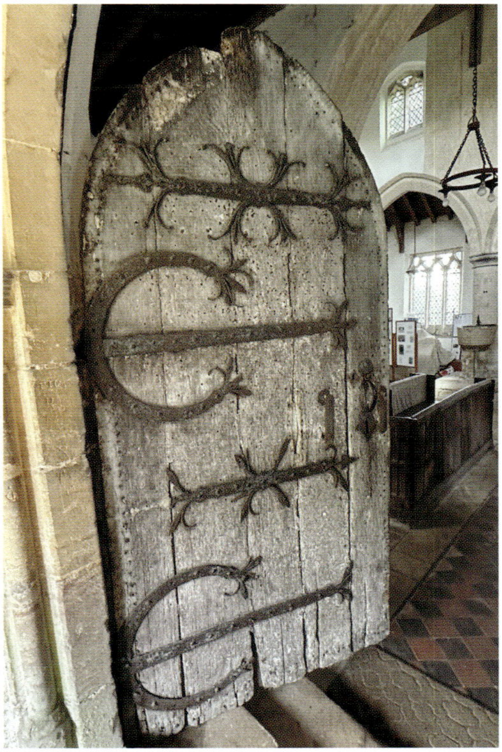

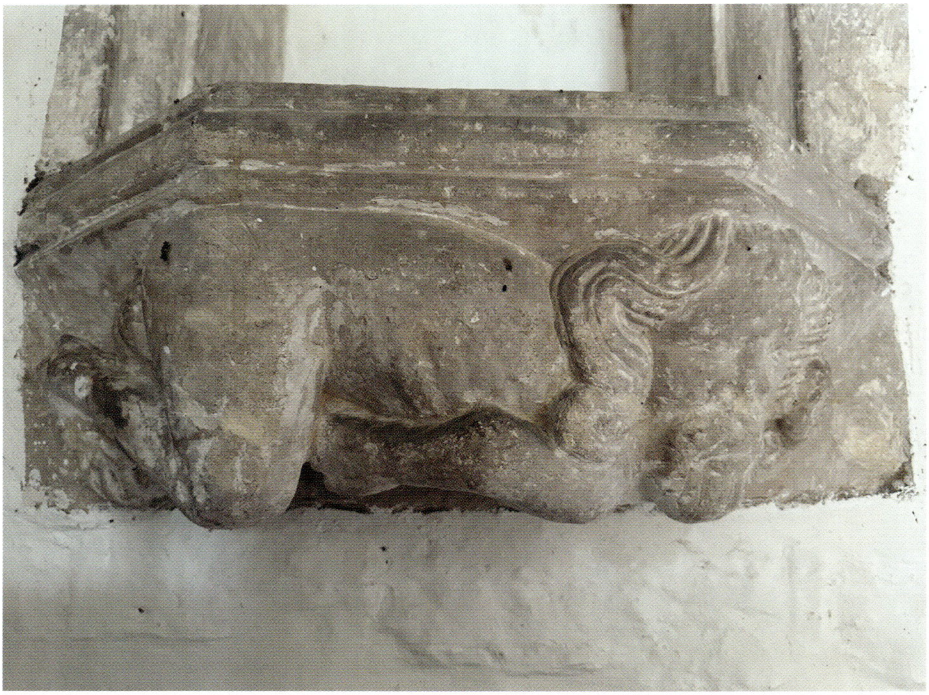

Pickworth. Beneath this piscina (the drain for the priest to wash holy vessels) is an image of a naked man. It may well represent the man who donated it.

If you look up at this point it is possible to see the mortice holes underneath the chancel arch where the wooden tympanum above the rood loft would have been fixed. My favourite feature, however, is in the south aisle where the piscina (the drain for the priest to wash the vessels at Mass) is supported by a bearded man with wavey hair. It's not until you realise that he is naked and wonder where his right hand is going that you realise this is a play on the name piscina!

37. Quadring, St Margaret

This little-known church stands away from its village next to the school and you'll need to make prior arrangements to visit it. Here is a fourteenth-century church remodelled within 100 years of its construction with splendid arcades of the fifteenth century, where the castellated attached columns are set within deeply moulded arches. They must have had a wealthy patron. On the south side of the chancel arch is an unusual internal stair turret to the rood loft rather than the usual staircase in the wall, although it is remarkably short compared to the height of the church. The nave roof is fifteenth century, so the prominent date of 1698 can only refer to a repair under the churchwardens whose initials, 'IC' and 'NP', are clearly recorded. The chancel is mainly nineteenth century. At the back of the church the font is a shadow of its former self, although its base has an inscription in Latin recording its donor, Robert Percy, and it is probably the same date as the

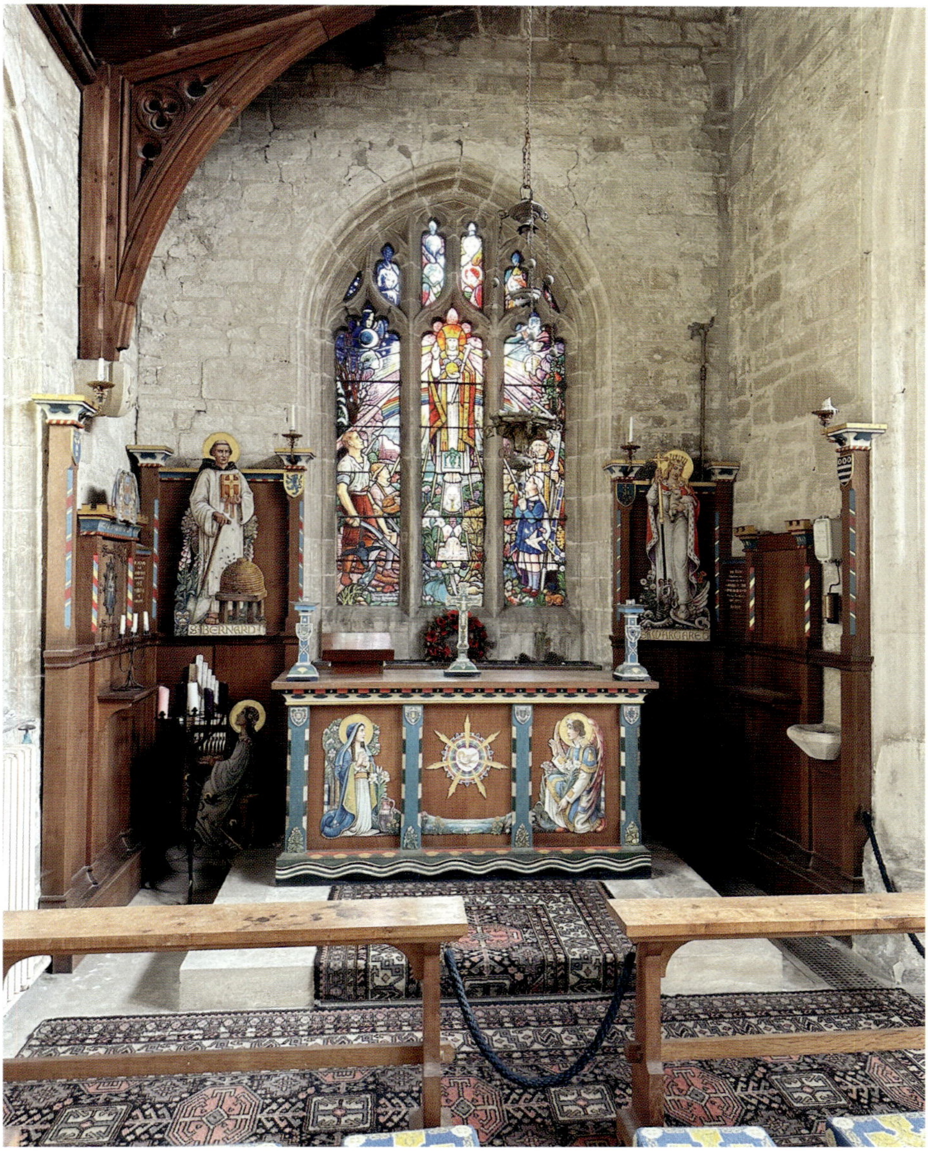

Quadring. The north-east chapel is a riot of twentieth-century design by father and son team Albert and Peter Lemmon of the Bromsgrove Guild, and is quite unexpected in an otherwise unremarkable building.

arcades. Nearby is something older, a dome-lidded chest, one of several dozen in the country imported from the Baltic during the late medieval period and most commonly found in the eastern counties of England. The outstanding furnishings here are the twentieth-century embellishments in the north aisle, which include windows, altar and reredos designed by father and son Albert and Peter Lemmon of the Bromsgrove Guild. It is a complete period piece and as such is one of the treasures of Lincolnshire. The east window depicts Christ in Majesty with contemporary figures of the 1940s below. There is attention to detail everywhere with the night, the winds, planets, ploughs and even parsnips to discover. Beneath it is a reredos with painted panels depicting St Margaret, St Bernard, St Cecilia and Our Lady of Walsingham, and the candlesticks and cross form part of the same set. The latter could easily be overlooked but it shows a naked Christ, with no beard, his body entwined by pomegranates, a favourite symbol in the Arts and Crafts movement from William Morris onwards. The altar depicts the Annunciation, with the Holy Spirit depicted as a dove in a full circle rainbow above a lily pond. The north aisle windows, by the same father and son team, depict Biblical scenes set against clear glass – and it is with clear glass that we end our visit to Quadring. In the south aisle the clear glass is old and two of the windows are scratched with graffiti left by glaziers. One records 'D Gemy of Ely 1793' whilst the easternmost window on the south side has this doggerel, 'Hear I ham booth day and night. To keep out cold an let in lite.'

38. Redbourne, St Andrew

The tall tower of St Andrew's is clearly of two different builds. The lower two storeys are medieval, whilst the top two storeys are eighteenth century and are constructed of much finer, coursed limestone rubble. They were added so that the church could be seen from the big house. Inside we are presented with a fascinating contrast of fourteenth-century arcades under a Georgian vaulted ceiling. The rubble walls are only lightly coated in limewash so that the texture shows through, and the starkness of the light interior is tempered by some very colourful stained glass and by green and red chevrons painted on the piers. The former are probably by the London glass maker William Collins, and demonstrate the use of orange glass so beloved by the period. It is Gothic in form and without the heaviness of the later nineteenth century. The Apostles are all named. Of rather greater intensity is the east window, also made by Collins. It shows the Last Day of Judgement, and we know here that it was designed by Francis Danby (d. 1861), an Irish artist known for his dramatic scenes. At the base is the Lamb of God, complete with the newly opened sixth seal (from the Book of Revelation). The other colour in the church is more recent and is the work of Revd Tremearne, who tried to make the church more 'fit for purpose' in the first half of the twentieth century. His chevrons are medieval in concept and work well, but his other paintwork, for example on the pulpit and west door, has little precedent. Tremearne became a national figure as he battled against the congregation here. He covered up the east window and accused the congregation of living in the past. His moves were unpopular amongst the old guard, but encouraged new attendees. In the chancel is a fourteenth-century, incised Tournai marble slab effigy of Sir Gerard Soothill (Clothill; d. 1410), set onto a stone table tomb beneath a cusped arch. Kneeling angels hold his visor open. Most of the other monuments in the church relate to the Beauclerk family, Dukes of St Albans, whose vault is to the south of the chancel and who married into the local Carter family. The most famous member of the family is remembered by a memorial by Sir Francis Chantry. Harriot Mellon

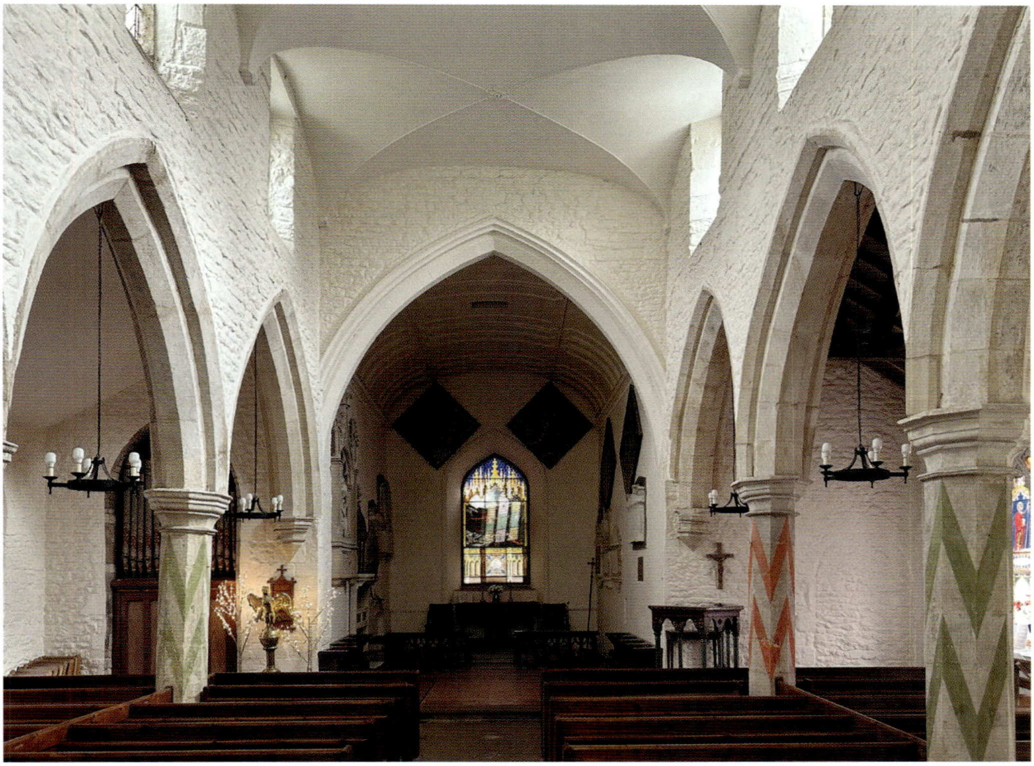

Above: Redbourne. Interior looking east, where we can see several prominent remodels of the medieval church. The chancel was rebuilt in 1772, the east window glazed in 1840 and the piers painted in chevrons by the eccentric incumbent Revd Tremane in the twentieth century.

Right: Redbourne. The centrepiece of the 1840 east window depicts the Lamb of God from the Book of Revelation sitting on the seven seals that hold the judgements from God at the end of days.

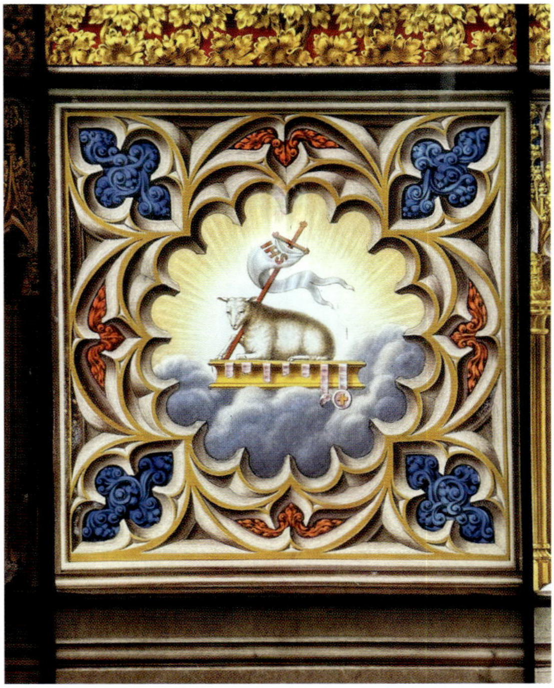

was a famous actress who married Thomas Coutts the banker. After his death she married the Duke of St Albans, thus becoming a duchess. Interestingly, her fortune did not go to the Beauclerk family. She left it to her step-granddaughter, Angela Burdett-Coutts.

39. Saltfleetby, All Saints

Seemingly remote from the world, this part of Lincolnshire has many churches of interest, but All Saints is the church of choice for the dedicated 'church crawler' who likes to discover little details and who relishes the atmosphere of old churches. This area was once a busy port which brought in money for the construction of such an impressive building. As you approach the church from the south its leaning tower is the most obvious feature, the result of settlement in the soft ground. At neighbouring St Peter's Church they tried to adjust the lean on the tower, but here they could only build bigger and bigger buttresses to try to stop it falling. The church is roofed with lead, but the chancel displays a slate roof, reminding us that this part of the church was under the ownership of the patron until 100 years ago. The Tudor brick porch carries an inscription in limestone above the door recording its donor, John Grantham of Moulton, and you step down into a large, light-filled space of nave, aisles, chancel and south chapel. The floor is unrestored so contains a selection of tiles, bricks, ledger stones and early monuments, the largest of which is the plain coffin-shaped slab just inside the chancel. The screens are a

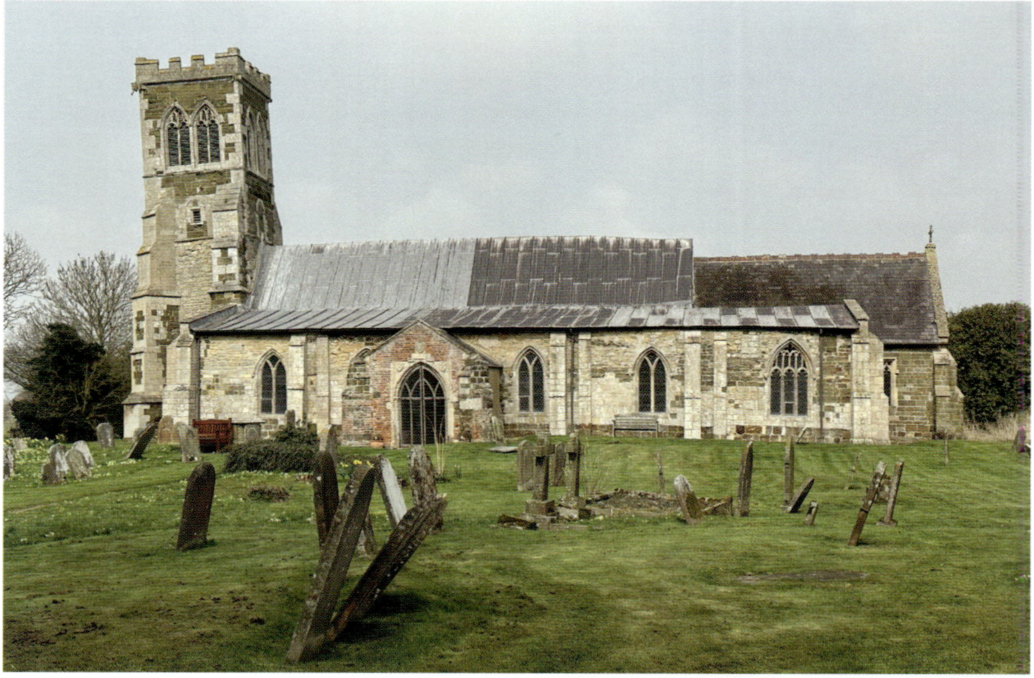

Saltfleetby. The tower has a tremendous lean due to the soft soil. It is a charmingly rustic building with patched-up walls and roofs.

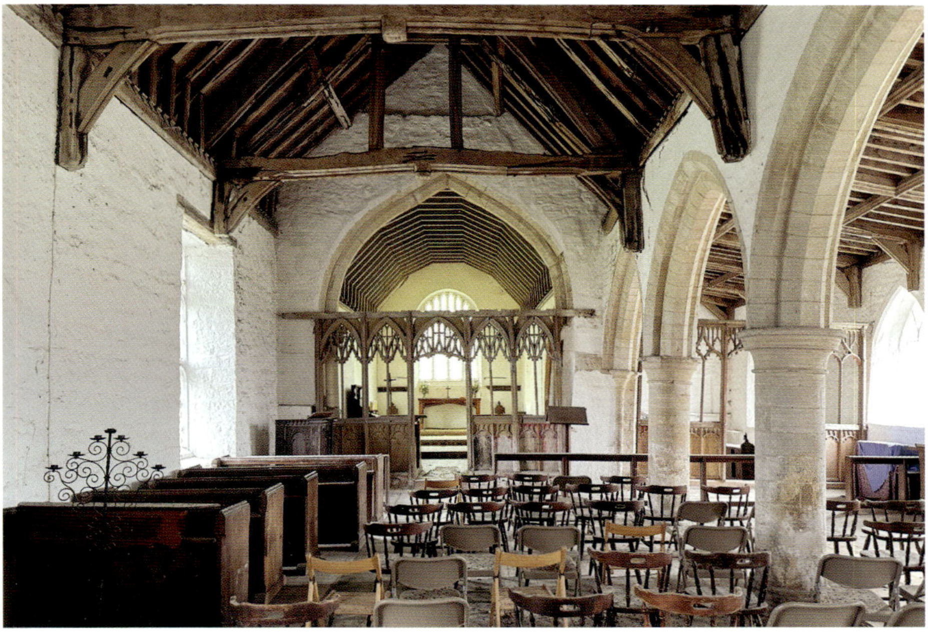

Saltfleetby. Interior looking east, showing the thirteenth-century piers leading to the south aisle. Whilst it looks a good fit, the rood screen has been brought in from another church.

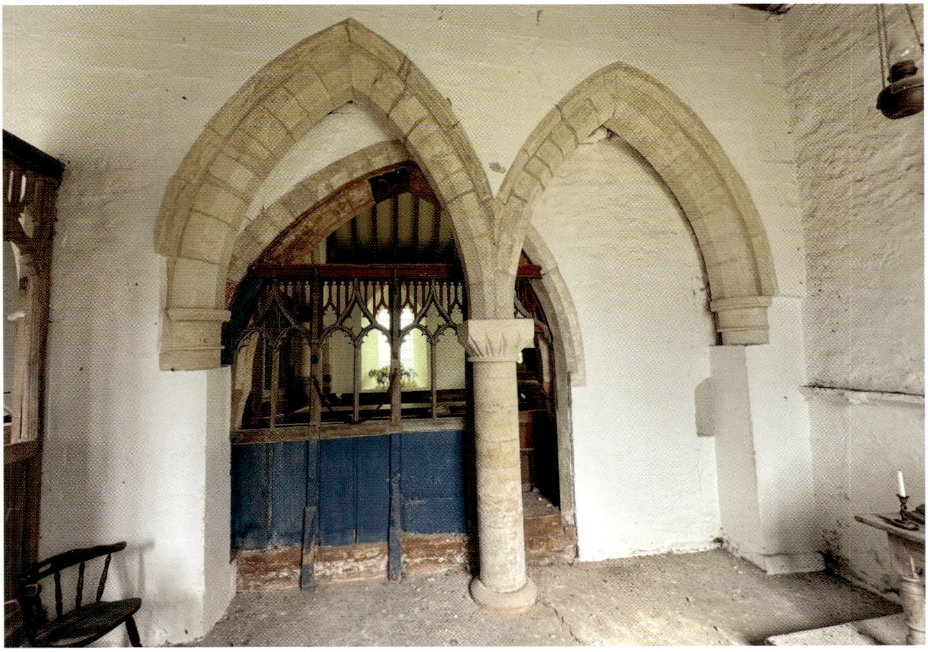

Saltfleetby. In the thirteenth century a start was made on beautifying and extending their church. Here a new single arch was constructed to link chancel and south chapel, but the work remained unfinished and the earlier two arches were left in situ.

particular feature of the building, although the impressive chancel screen has come from another church – you can see that it is too wide and the notches in the chancel arch show where the original screen would have slotted in. Nonetheless, it is an impressive piece with some remaining red and green paintwork. The easternmost window in the chancel south wall has had its sill cut down to form a sedilia – or seat – for the clergy at Mass. Between the chancel and south chapel there is something of an architectural puzzle. In the chapel is a Romanesque pier with scalloped capital which supports a pair of later pointed arches. Soon after this was completed it was decided to join the chapel and chancel with a single arch instead. The puzzle comes when we try to guess why they didn't complete the job and demolish the earlier pair of arches. Perhaps the ground was unstable or money ran out. The same reason may explain the fact that the space under the tower was originally due to be stone vaulted. The ribs survive but led nowhere, suggesting that this project too was abandoned. For many years the south chapel was used as a vestry but is now restored as a chapel with a delicate fourteenth-century reredos in its east wall, its pinnacles sitting on two heads in an almost comedy and tragedy pairing. Other faces may be found supporting the font where four devilish faces are having their life extinguished by the weight of the font and its sacramental purpose.

40. Scotton, St Genewys

The north doorway acts as a prelude to the architectural glories of this church as it is a high-quality textbook example of thirteenth-century architecture with a pointed arch, two sets of shafts and deeply carved dogtooth decoration. You enter an enormous church, full of light and architectural promise. The north arcade has circular piers and is contemporary with the door, whilst the south

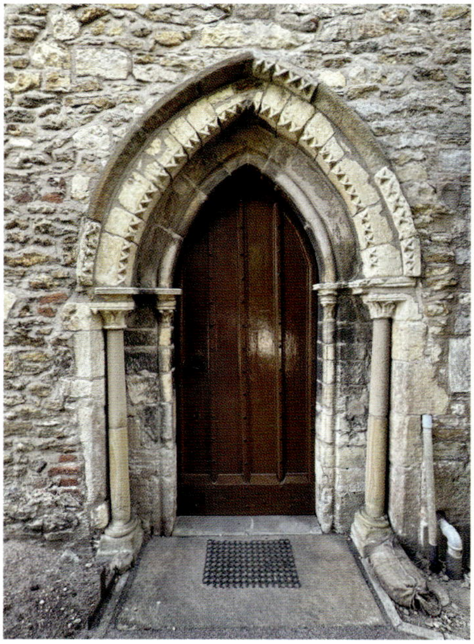

Scotton. This fine north doorway dates from the early thirteenth century when we were using the new pointed Gothic form of architecture but hadn't quite let go of the decorative aspects of Romanesque styles – hence the dogtooth carving.

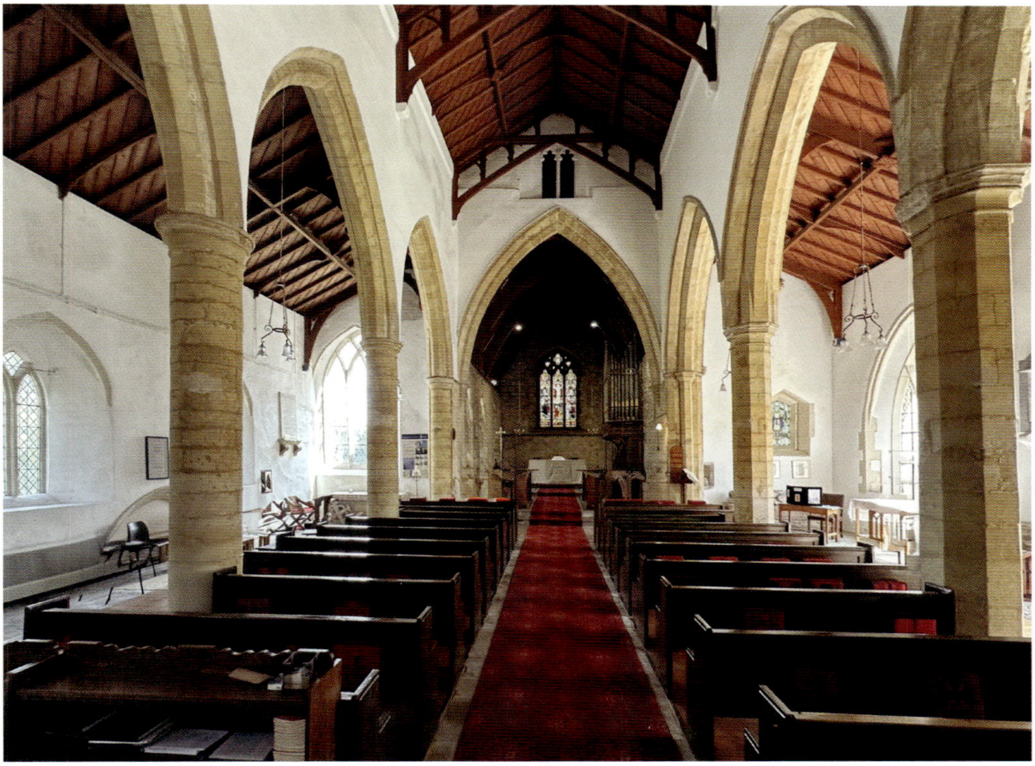

Above: Scotton. Here the north arcade with its circular piers predates the south arcade by about fifty years. On the left you can pick out a tomb recess, which probably marks the grave of the person who paid for the north aisle.

Right: Scotton. This fine head-and-shoulders monument from the late thirteenth century now sits in the north aisle, but as it depicts a priest it would originally have been in the chancel, which was cleared out in 1866.

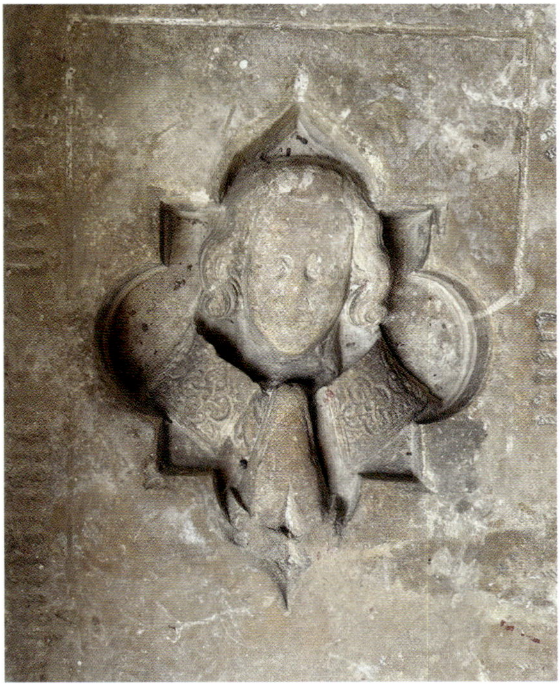

arcade is a generation or two later with octagonal piers. Whoever paid for the early work probably lies under the arched recess in the north aisle where there is an incomplete inscription carved in Lombardic letters. The roofline of the earliest phase of building can be picked out against the tower wall. At the east end of the north aisle is a fine head-and-shoulders effigy of a priest dating from the first half of the fifteenth century. His apparelled amice has especially fine detail consisting of a row of quatrefoils. This high-quality monument is in stark contrast to the crudely scratched 'SP 1718' on a stone nearby. There was originally an altar in the south aisle as a blocked hole at the east end once led to the chancel and would have given a priest in the aisle a view of his colleague at the high altar. Beneath it is a thirteenth-century, cross-legged knight wearing chain mail and lying on a later, much renewed, tomb chest. Above it is a twentieth-century window with a depiction of the church in the background together with a good crop of root vegetables. The chancel was restored by the renowned architect George Edmund Street in 1866 and has a very Victorian feel. The walls have been stripped of plaster, making it markedly darker than the rest of the church. On the south side the windowsill has been dropped to form a simple sedile – very much in keeping with the date of the original church. The font is also Victorian, with a pillar of coloured marble and the symbol of the Holy Trinity around its bowl. Other writers have been sniffy about it, but it matches the architecture of the church perfectly. Outside, it is clear to see that the tower has been heightened, probably in the fifteenth century when bells started to be hung on wheels, and that the south aisle has been rebuilt to run the length of the nave only and not to clasp the tower where the blocked arch shows that it originally stood.

41. Sleaford, St Denys

For much of its history Sleaford was a prosperous town, benefitting firstly from agriculture and later industry. This explains the character of the church, which is created by both impressive medieval architecture and by nineteenth- and twentieth-century restorations. The view from the south is fascinating, with fourteenth-century windows of the south aisle of varying tracery, above which the clerestory windows and pinnacles of the fifteenth-century rebuilding cannot compete. No wonder the Victorian church restorers countrywide favoured the styles first used in the fourteenth century when looking for their inspiration. The church fronts the tiny marketplace. A study of the west end shows that it is not a symmetrical building, but one which evolved and grew around the early thirteenth-century tower. Set back a little is an outer north aisle, added in 1853. The familiar fourteenth-century piers that are a hallmark of churches in this part of the county are here very much taller than usual and take the eye down the church until it is abruptly stopped by the rood loft, beyond which it is difficult to see into the chancel. The screen is a work of 1918 by Sir Ninian Comper, and very fine it is too, incorporating most of an original screen. Comper wanted the old and new work to be read as one piece so, unusually, he kept his work to a restrained plain wood. The original doorways to the rood loft survive, so as a whole it gives us a good impression of how a medieval screen and loft worked. In

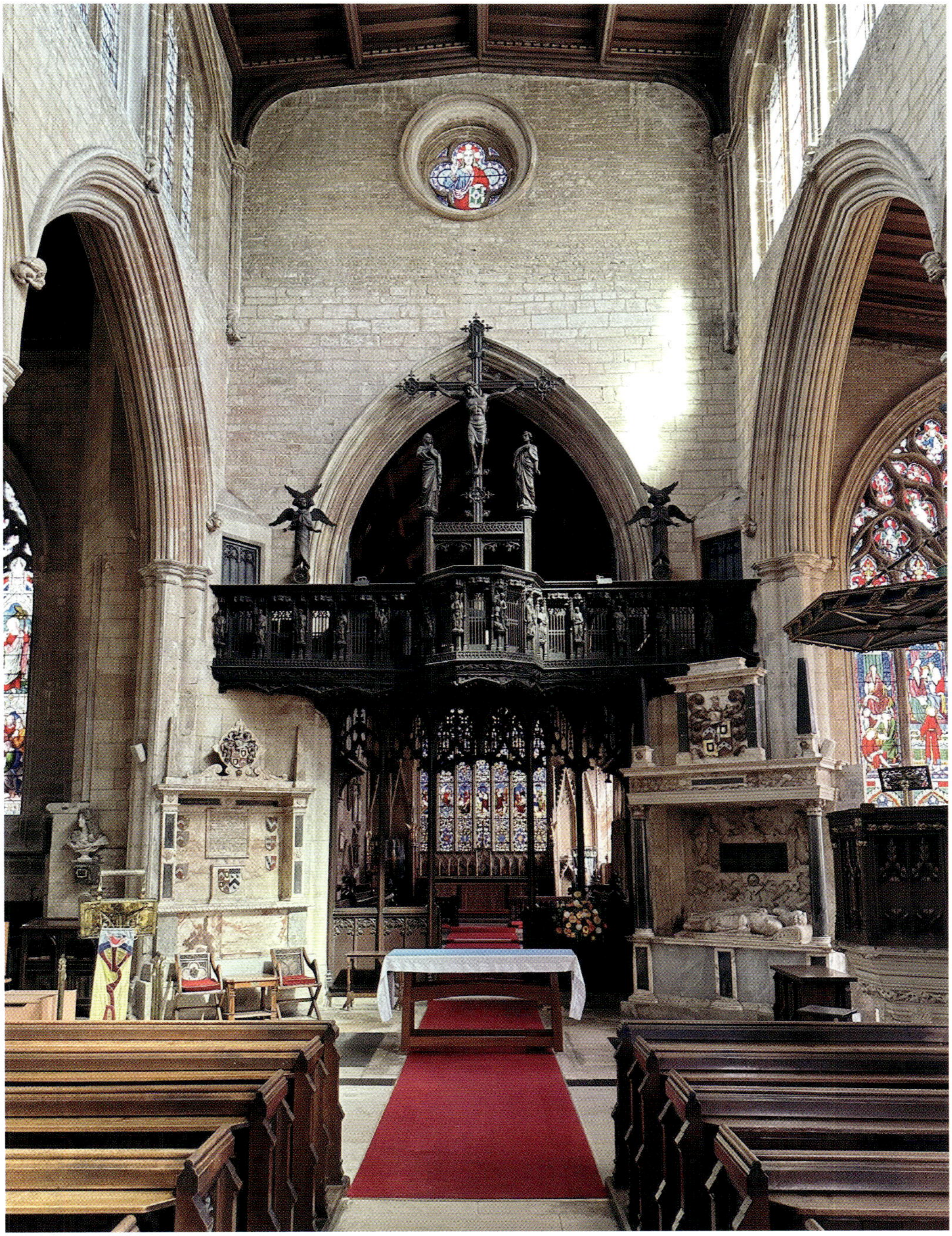

Sleaford. A stately civic church which shows the wealth of the town in the fourteenth century. The interior is dominated by the rood screen. The base is mainly medieval, but the rood loft and rood figures above are twentieth century, designed by the great Sir Ninian Comper to exactly the same scale as their medieval predecessors.

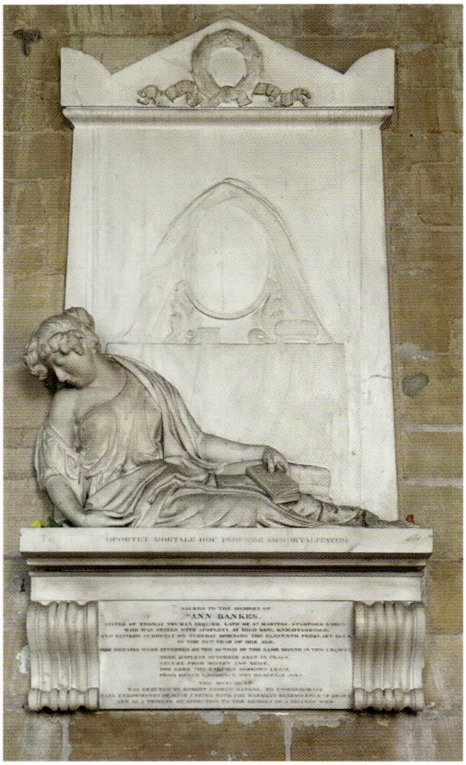

Sleaford. The monument to Ann Bankes (d. 1834) is by Sir Richard Westmacott. It records her death from a sudden attack of apoplexy on the north side of Knightsbridge.

front of the screen are two post-Reformation alabaster monuments, both to the Carr family, and displaying their shield of arms on the entablature. The northern one, to Robert Carr (d. 1590), has no effigy and is based solely on his heraldry and that of his two wives, whilst the other monument to his son Edward (d. 1618) is more impressive with effigies of both him and his wife. Interestingly, she survived him and went on to marry Oliver Cromwell's uncle, which may be why the figures are badly damaged. In the chancel is a white marble memorial to Ann Bankes sculpted by Sir Richard Westmacott, who, the inscription records, was 'seized with apoplexy' on the north side of Knightsbridge in 1834. The young lady seen declining on the memorial was most certainly not a portrait of the deceased, who was at least fifty years older than the model portrayed. As you leave the church via the north aisle you'll notice that at the west end an X-shaped brace was inserted in 1853 to stop the tower leaning to the north.

42. Snarford, St Lawrence

Sometimes the least promising of churches gives us a surprise. Here the diminutive church with its tiny thirteenth-century tower and its unadorned exterior hides a set of three important monuments to the St Paul family, who purchased the big house here in the fifteenth century. They must have seen this as a big step up from their Yorkshire home, but it was just the start of things as 100 years later they became powerful as a result of investing in land previously owned by the monasteries, and with that newfound wealth they could arrange important marriages. By the mid sixteenth century we were a Protestant nation, and altars had been removed from our chancels, but there was still the possibility that they might be brought back. This is why the large monument to Sir Thomas St Paul (d. 1582) was erected in the centre of the chancel, where the altar once stood. It shows that he was a determined Protestant. The monument takes the form of a six-poster alabaster canopy over Thomas and his wife Faith. There is heraldry galore – look out for the lovely elephant at his helm. On top of the canopy are their daughters, whilst on the pedestal above you can see their son and heir George. The paintwork has been conserved. George appears again on the tall monument against the north wall of the chapel, where he lies on a shelf above an effigy of his wife Frances. Sadly, their only child, a daughter named Mattathia, died young and is shown at the base attended by two mourning cherubs. After George's death Frances became quite a catch and married Robert, Lord Rich, future Earl of Warwick. They are portrayed together on the wall monument in the north chapel; he proudly looks out to the viewer while she, wearing her coronet as a countess, looks to the right. It may have been designed by the sculptor Epiphanius Evesham, whose career gave us

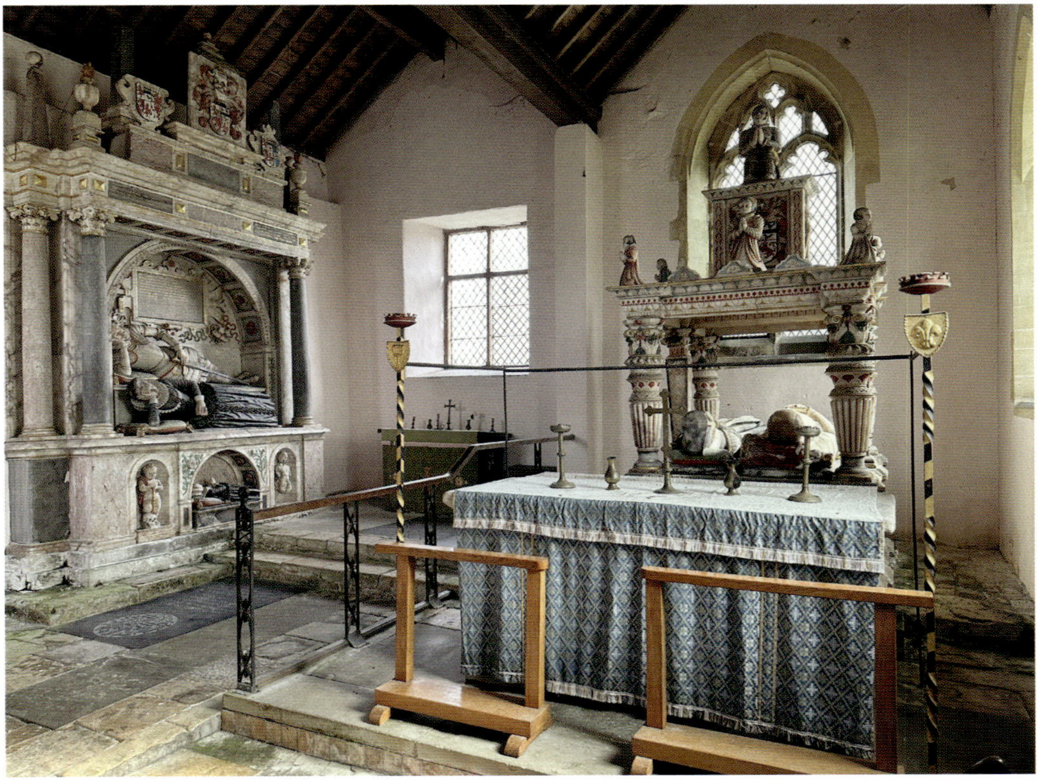

Snarford. This church contains a number of monuments of national importance. Behind the altar is that to Sir Thomas St Paule (d. 1582), whilst against the north wall we find Sir George St Paul (d. 1613).

some of the most lifelike effigies of their date. Apart from the effigies, the font is worth a careful inspection. It was likely a gift of the St Paul family when they first came here, which is why the iconography of the symbols of the Passion were not damaged after the Reformation. The head of Christ is particularly powerful. It must have looked splendid in its original painted form.

43. Snitterby, St Nicholas

James Fowler is a name we come across time and again when visiting Lincolnshire churches. He was Diocesan Surveyor and responsible for the restoration of many medieval churches in the county. He also designed new churches, and this is one of his finest, dating from 1866. The exterior is of rock-faced limestone which is laid in horizontal courses, and there is an apsidal chancel in the style of the mid-thirteenth century. Fowler built his new church against the base of a surviving medieval tower, but this eventually collapsed and was replaced by the present tower in 1894. Fowler was nothing if not inventive, as we discover on going inside. Here we find a completely brick-built church with the use of decorative polychromy. Of special note are the windows which have rere-arches at their heads – again, picked out in coloured brick. These just create a three-dimensional

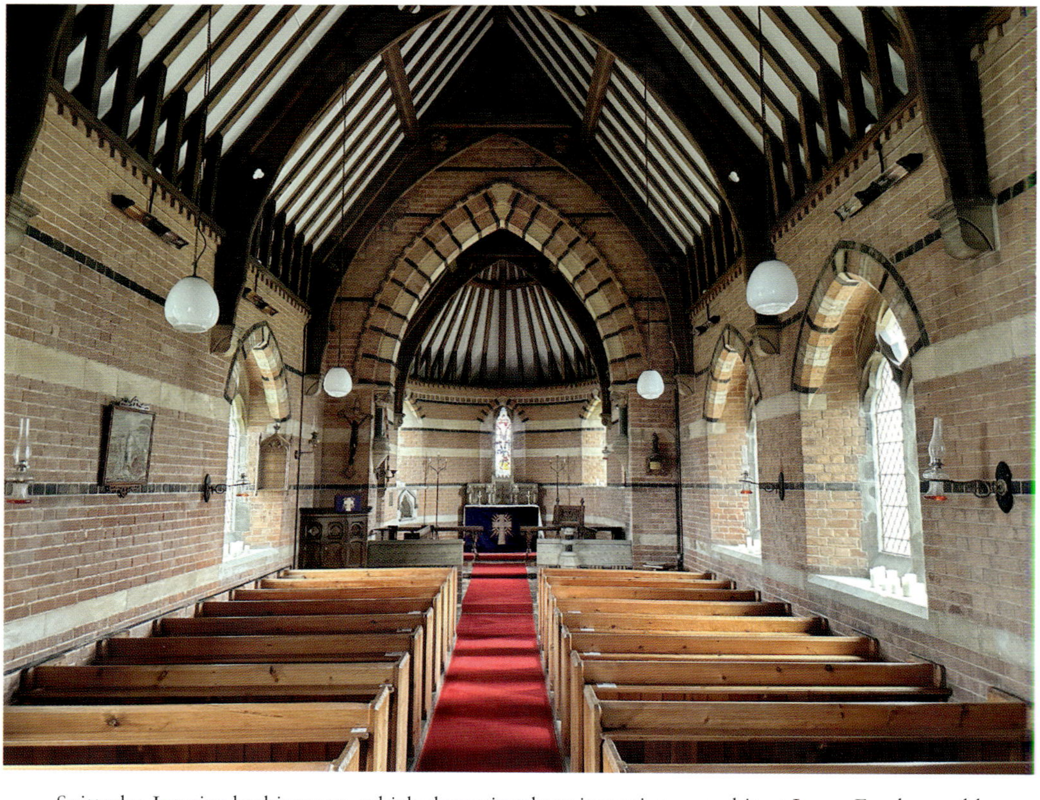

Snitterby. Interior looking east, which shows just how inventive an architect James Fowler could be. Built in 1866 with much use of polychromatic bricks to create a rich interior.

look to the windows and mirror in brick – what a medieval church may have had in limestone. There is a low wall dividing nave and chancel, its stone coping carved like a roof of fish-scale tiles, and on the south side it sprouts a wooden lectern supported on a black marble pedestal. The marble reredos incorporates a plain cross as this was one of the last churches to be built before it became legal to once again place a cross on the altar. In 1866, this was still illegal, so Fowler was adhering to the law. The standard of stone carving throughout is high. The limestone capitals are especially good with their acanthus leaf design. At the back of the church are some interesting artifacts, including a poster advertising the reopening of the church in 1894 and a drawing of the previous church, which Fowler determined to be too far gone to repair.

44. Spilsby, St James

Most churches show some work of the nineteenth century, when long-neglected buildings benefited from newly found wealth. But not all had as much money spent on them as Spilsby where the church was more than doubled in size, leaving a curious interior. We enter from the north into the north aisle of a fourteenth-century church. This leads into the nave, and there was originally a matching

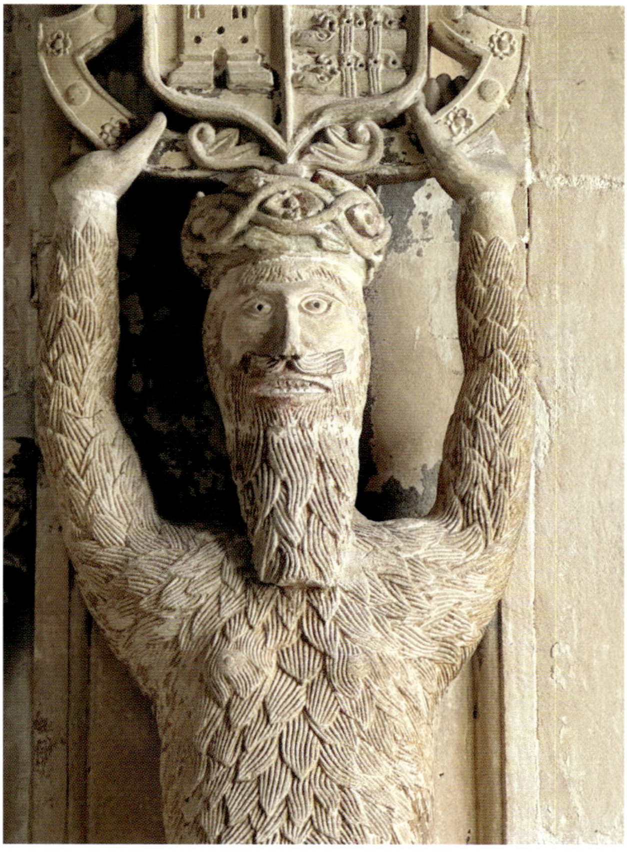

Spilsby. This 'wodewose', or wild man of the woods, which forms part of the family heraldry is on the huge Willoughby monument of 1580.

south aisle, too. However, this was soon replaced by a larger addition to form a new nave. A photograph of 1874 is displayed to show what the church looked like. Then in 1878 the architect William Bassett-Smith raised the nave walls and added the current south aisle, carefully matching the original architecture to the north. In the original church the arcades separating nave and aisles stopped short at the east end. This was to give room on top of the rood screen for the medieval loft to run the full width of the church. A full arch would have made it impossible for the sacristan to walk across the screen. Bassett-Smith replicated this on the south side to make sure everything matched. At the back of the church is a memorial to Spilsby's most famous son, Sir John Franklin (1784–1847), the Arctic explorer who died whilst attempting to navigate the Northwest Passage. Yet this is not the monument most visitors to the church come to see, for the north chapel is a veritable gallery of sculpted stone belonging to the Willoughby d'Eresby family. They date from the fourteenth to the seventeenth centuries and show how funerary monuments developed during that period. Similar recumbent effigies and memorial brasses may be found singly in other churches, but here they are trumped by the exceptional standing monument to the 12th Baroness Willoughby (1519–80), who held the title in her own right. Her head, and that of her husband, are both too small to be original to the monument, but the pilgrim, Saracen and wodewose from the Willoughby shield of arms are impossible to miss. Originally, they would have been brightly coloured and must have looked quite different.

45. Stamford, St Martin

The picturesque town of Stamford offers church crawlers rich pickings, with open churches seemingly on every corner. St Martin's Church stands to the south of the River Welland, its tower dominating the main road into the town from the south. Setting it apart from others in Stamford is its connection with Burghley House, the big local estate, with monuments to the owners, the Cecil family. The church is entered through a vaulted porch, the central boss of which displays the shield of arms of the diocese of Lincoln and leads into a building almost entirely rebuilt in the late 1400s, although it has a very Victorian feel following major refurbishment in 1844. The box pews date from this time and were built in oak to the designs of a local builder. On the book rest by each pew door is a small brass card holder to remind us that these seats were rented; the name of those allowed to use them were prominently displayed. The benches around the aisle walls were allocated to the use of the poor. The underfloor heating introduced in the nineteenth century has been discontinued but the gratings have been saved and, though closed with concrete, the elaborate ironwork is still visible. The windows give us the story of the development of Victorian glass, but in the south-east corner and in the east window we see something much more important: a range of medieval glass fragments. It is believed that these came from Tattershall Church (see entry 47) in the eighteenth century. The north chapel was rebuilt as the burial vault of the Cecil family and most visitors come to see the monument to William Cecil (d. 1598), the 1st Lord Burghley and famous as Queen Elizabeth I's chief minister. It is certainly a statement piece in painted alabaster. Behind, in the chapel, is a monument to his

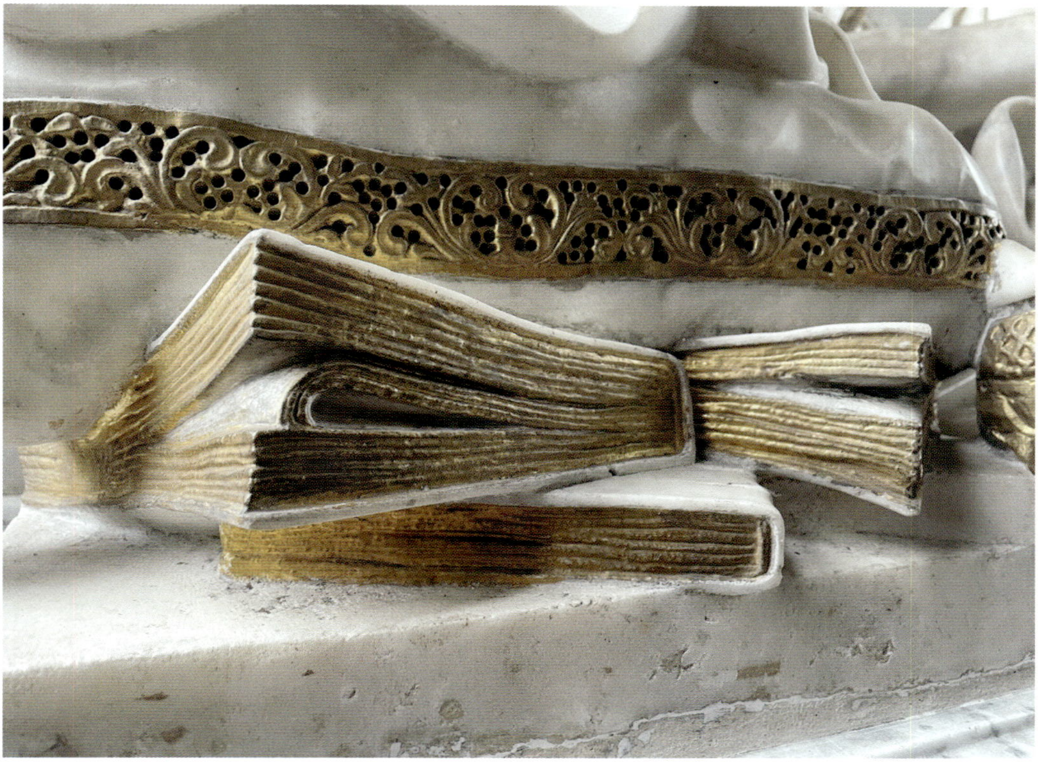

Stamford. The monument to John Cecil, 5th Earl of Exeter (d. 1700) incorporates this pile of books to show his learning. He went on three grand tours of the Continent, purchasing hundreds of works of art.

parents, Richard and Jane, and their three daughters. Yet both these monuments pale into insignificance against the startling white marble confection designed by an Italian sculptor to commemorate the 5th Earl of Exter (d. 1700), which depicts him in antique Roman costume within a monumental architectural setting. In the floor nearby is the entrance to the Cecil vault and, surprisingly, a memorial tablet to Prime Minister Benjamin Disraeli (d. 1881), who was a close friend and colleague of the 3rd Marquess of Exeter. In the churchyard extension is the grave of Daniel Lambert (d. 1809), one of the heaviest people in England who earned a living displaying himself to the public. He weighed over 52 stone and twenty men were required to carry his coffin.

46. Stoke Rochford, St Mary and St Andrew

Less than a mile from the Great North Road, this outstanding church highlights the fine arts of centuries. The building itself is of Norman origin, enlarged on several occasions, especially by the addition of chapels to the chancel in the fifteenth century. These belonged to the two major families of the area and contains their monuments and those to their predecessors, moved here from elsewhere in the church. The oldest is the double effigy in the floor of the north chapel showing a couple lying in bed covered with a blanket with animals at their feet. Nearby is a splendid tomb recess which contains a chest tomb with five angels on its side, each holding a shield. They must once have been painted with the arms of the person commemorated. In the floor of the chancel (under the heavy carpet) are some late medieval brasses whilst the south chapel is dominated by the tall painted alabaster monument to Henry Cholmeley (d. 1641) his wife and children. In front of their rather crude effigies is a charming image of their granddaughter Mary who died at the age of just eighteen days. Later members of the family are remembered by panels along the base. The north chapel houses a white marble reredos to the memory of Christopher Turnor (d. 1886) and his wife. It shows the couple in portrait medallions with three Gothic towers containing images of early saints, including Augustine, Hilda, Bede and Margaret of Scotland. It is an extraordinary piece of bravura. The reredos in the chancel is also noteworthy, having been designed by Mary Seton Watts, artist wife of George Frederick Watts, in 1911. Better known for her amazing chapel at Compton in Surrey, the vine leaf trail along the top of the reredos is typical of her designs. It represents six saints, including St Hugh of Lincoln with his swan. Later in the twentieth century the church was further beautified by the artist Jessie Bayes, who came from a large family of notable Arts and Crafts artists. In 1935, she painted Christ in Majesty in the gap between the chancel roof and the chancel arch, and two years later Christopher Turnor commissioned the fine font cover from her. It consists of three tiers of fretwork panels each painted with a scene from the Life of Christ. She signed the panel which shows the Adoration of the Magi. In the churchyard is the grave of legendary strongman Geoff Capes (d. 2024).

47. Tattershall, Holy Trinity

In 1439, Ralph, Lord Cromwell, established a collegiate foundation here in a church next to the red-brick castle he was building. As Lord Treasurer of England, he had power and wealth and wished his two buildings to mirror his position. The castle still stands by the church, but the church was remodelled by William of Waynflete, his executor. It is a building of majestic proportions. The priests who lived here in a secular community were charged with praying for Cromwell's soul and for the souls of any other benefactor who left money for the purpose. They would have worshipped in the chancel, separated from the parishioners by a wooden rood screen. This was replaced by the present stone pulpitum in 1528, which included large recesses north and south for altars in the nave. Collegiate foundations were extremely popular places of burial, and the north transept contains a collection of brasses moved from elsewhere in the church, each person buried here believing that their donation meant that their souls would be prayed for by priests 'for ever'. Sadly, in 1547 collegiate foundations were declared illegal and the entire building became the parish church. The east window contains some of the best medieval glass in the country, dating from the late fifteenth century. Although it is now displayed in an arbitrary fashion, it would once have formed a narrative throughout the church. A panel to look out for depicts infant baptism

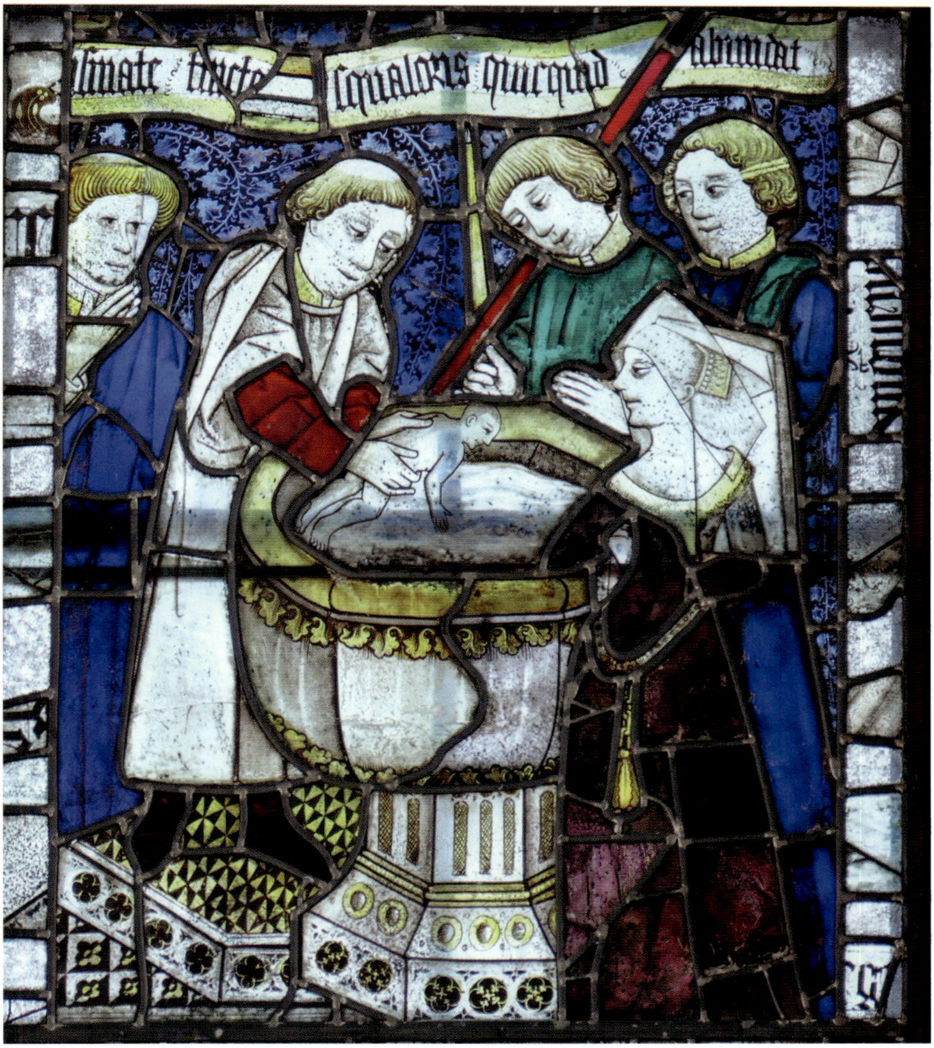

Tattershall. The finest medieval glass in the county is grouped in the east window. Dating from the last quarter of the fifteenth century, this panel represents baptism, where the baby is dipped into the font three times.

and shows the baby (more a miniature man) being dipped into the font, as was late medieval practice. Much glass which had survived the Reformation, was removed in the late eighteenth century and can be seen in Stamford (see entry 45) and in Burghley House. The panelled roof of the nave is heavy with oak, although not perhaps as grand as one might expect, with just a sprinkling of diminutive angels. A beautifully carved ledger stone to the local apothecary William Wright (d. 1735) records how he was a good all-rounder, his character 'acquired only by ye strength of his natural parts and unwearied industry'. Towards the back of the church is an intriguing small inscription in the floor to 'T Thumb died 1620'.

48. Waithe, St Martin

It is rare to find a church with two such contrasting displays of architecture, both of the highest quality. The church has a tall central tower of rectangular shape. It is not entirely clear whether the ground floor served as the nave of the original church, or if there was a smaller nave on the site of the present one. From the outside the tower is constructed of large blocks of stone, not quite smooth enough to be called ashlar. It may have been limewashed originally. The bell openings are typically eleventh century, around the time of the Norman Conquest. The parapet has obviously been repaired using ironstone. The church is entered through the Victorian south transept, where you are suddenly thrown into one of the gloomiest spaces imaginable. The Churches Conservation Trust, which now cares from the church, helpfully suggests you put on the lights. As it now stands the nave is entirely Victorian and built much taller than need be to match the proportions of the tower. It is the lack of a clerestory that makes it dark, an effect not helped by the banded bricks and flints of which it is built. Quotations run along the top of the walls. The east wall of the nave has a round-headed arch leading to the space under the tower where Fowler just managed to tuck some choir stalls in – and then another arch leads into the chancel. This really is the finest space; the

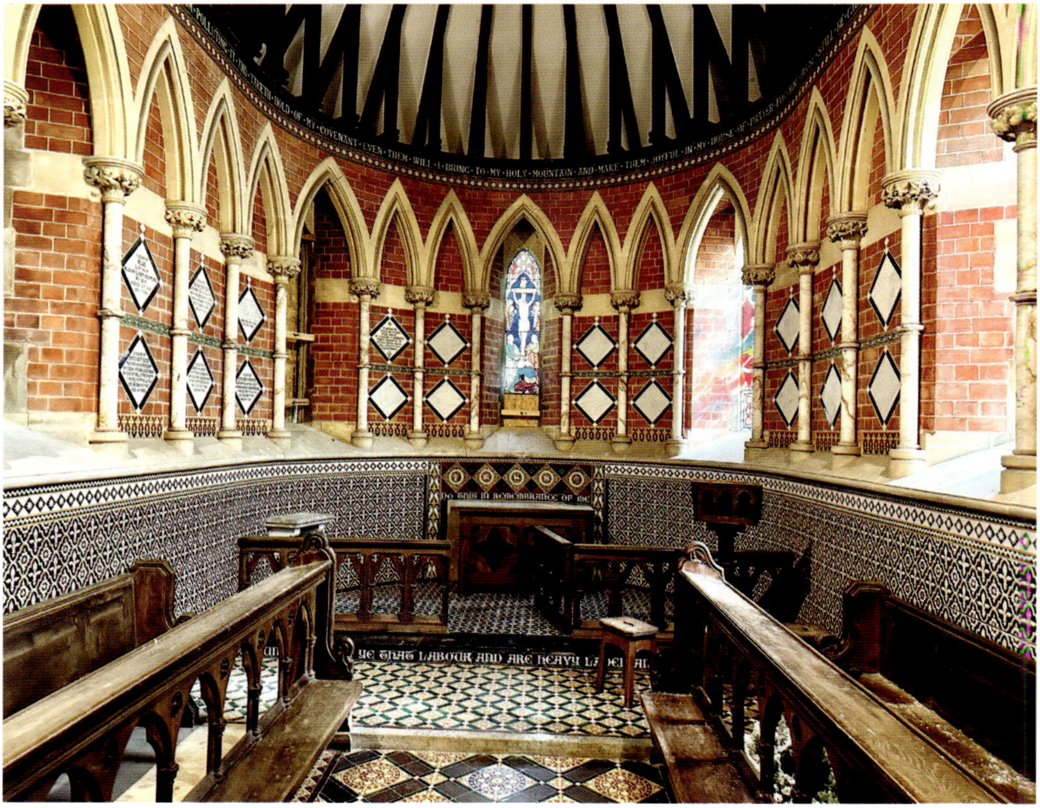

Waithe. A Saxon church with a heavy Victorian overlay including numerous Minton tiles paid for by the local squire and executed by Fowler of Louth.

lower walls are entirely lined with encaustic tiles made by the firm of Minton. Blind arcading covers the upper area, each arch being home to two plaques, those on the north side commemorating members of the Haigh family in whose memory the church was rebuilt. The reredos has Minton tiles showing the symbols of the Four Evangelists and the Lamb of God. When your eyes have got used to the gloom, leave what John Betjeman referred to as a 'public lavatory' and return to the nave to appreciate the hand-painted roll of honour from the First World War and the tub-shaped font, a Victorian interpretation of a Romanesque design.

49. West Keal, St Helen

There can be no better sited church in the county, its fourteenth-century stone-roofed porch providing the perfect frame for the view south to Boston and Norfolk. Both the chancel and the tower are Victorian rebuilds – the former by eminent architect George Edmund Street of 1867. Inside it has a stone roll moulding, which thirteenth-century churches often used, and which was a favourite device of Street in his restorations and rebuilds. It helped create a horizontal divide on the wall, emphasising its verticality. The plate tracery of the windows is unusual

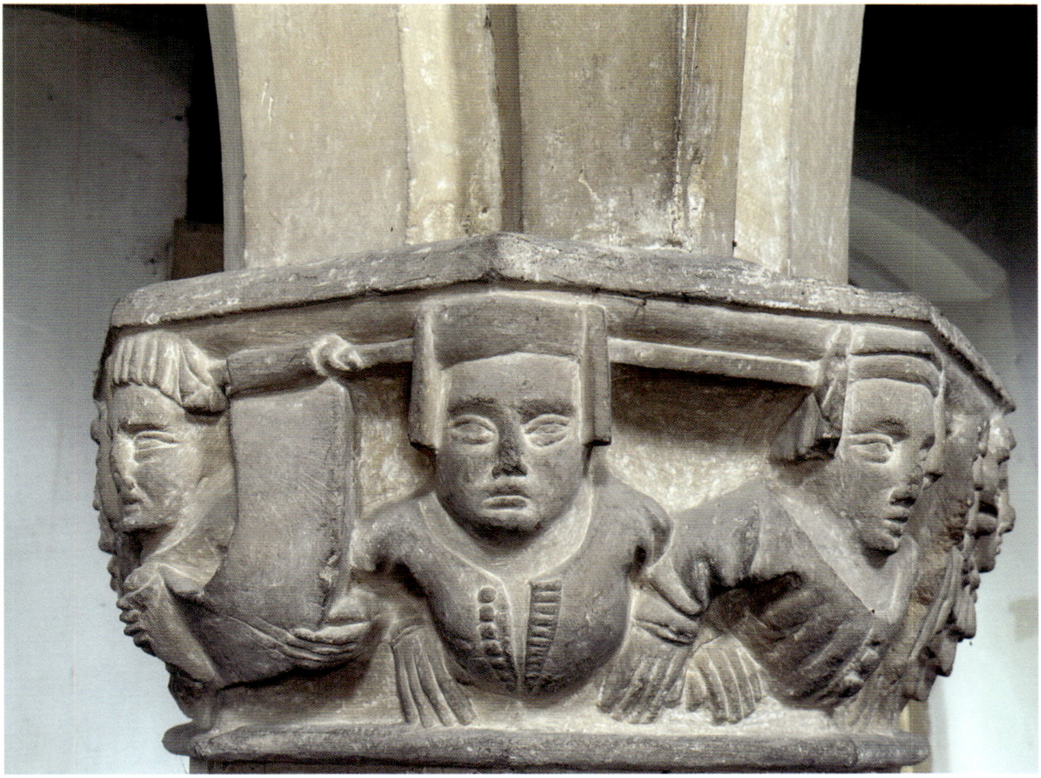

West Keal. The arcades have carved capitals of unique design. Here we see a group of women with their arms interlinked. On the left is a man with a scroll, which would probably have been painted with their names.

in Lincolnshire and certainly stands out against the bar tracery so usually found. The tower was a gift from the patron to replace the medieval tower, which collapsed in 1881. It is built of the local sandstone with Ancaster stone dressings. The nave is fourteenth century, now lit by fifteenth-century clerestory windows which throw light onto the outstanding carved capitals of the arcades. There is no other church like it in the county, with a series of individual carvings which seem to have been the whim of the individual craftsmen as there is no single theme to follow. For much of its history the church was in the patronage of Croyland Abbey in the Fens, so it was probably their money and stonemasons at work here. One image shows a fox with a goose in its mouth together with a chained monkey, while another has two fighting monsters. We can also find bearded men peeping out of foliage and women with entwined arms, which Sir John Betjeman recalled are 'almost bursting from their bodices'. At the back of the church is a weathered board recording the church fees in the nineteenth century, when ringing the bell cost 1*s* or double if it was for someone from outside the parish. The north aisle is built against the slope of the hillside, and this has obviously caused damp problems in the past, so a masonry 'skirt' has been added along the north aisle. Sadly, it has not been effective. Before you leave look at the piscina near the door. It cannot have been a holy water stoup as it has a drain, so must have been moved from elsewhere, probably from the chancel when it was rebuilt. The drain itself is formed from the face of a cat, one of several similar faces to be discovered inside the church. Medieval stonemasons loved to have fun.